500
appetisers

500

appetisers

Susannah Blake

APPLE

A Quintet Book

First published in the UK in 2007 by Apple Press
Sheridan House
114 Western Road
Hove
East Sussex
BN3 1DD

641·812

www.apple-press.com

ISBN: 978-1-84543-174-7
QUIN.LCOC

This book was designed and produced by
Quintet Publishing Limited
6 Blundell Street
London N7 9BH

Senior Editor: Ruth Patrick
Editor: Bridget Jones
Art Director: Dean Martin
Photography: Ian Garlick
Designer: Janis Utton
Home Economist: Wendy Sweetser
Creative Director: Richard Dewing
Publisher: Gaynor Sermon

10 9 8 7 6 5 4 3 2 1

Manufactured in Singapore by Pica Digital Pte Ltd.
Printed in China by SNP Leefung Printers Ltd.

contents

introduction

Appetisers can be wonderfully varied and still do exactly what their title says they will – their purpose is to whet the appetite and stimulate the tastebuds. Whether it's the simplest bowl of salted nuts to nibble with pre-dinner drinks, elegant cocktail canapés to accompany sophisticated aperitifs, or a stunning starter to savour at the table, they all share the same function. They should make the mouth water, encourage guests to relax and help to create a convivial atmosphere. They are also there to stave off possible hunger pangs until the main event, but be aware that appetisers should never spoil the appetite. Instead, they should tease it lightly by offering a stimulating foretaste of the culinary delights to come.

international appetisers

All over the world, there are countless bite-size morsels that serve as appetisers. Some are traditionally served as snacks between meals but work perfectly in the pre-meal role, while others have always been served as little taste-tempters. From France come the tiniest of appetisers – amuse bouches – miniature mouthfuls to play with everyone's hunger even before the appetiser arrives. Usually beautifully presented, these morsels range from mini crostini to a spoonful of soup to flirt with your tastebuds.

Also from France there are the classic hors d'oeuvres, traditionally a selection of small portions – usually cold – served at the beginning of a meal. Hors d'oeuvres may include anything from charcuterie and salad vegetables to smoked fish, anchovies and olives presented on a single platter or board.

The Italians have a similar first-course tradition known as antipasti, literally meaning "before pasta". This can include the simplest bruschetta with garlic and olive oil or a whole array of delicious savouries to try, such as crisp golden polenta, crostini topped with creamy mushrooms, marinated char-grilled vegetables, a simple mozzarella, tomato and basil salad, stuffed mussels, and wafer-thin slices of prosciutto.

Russians enjoy zakusi, literally meaning "little bites" and originally referring to sweet delicacies served after a meal, but now describing savouries served before the meal, often with vodka. These may include salted and pickled fish, caviar, sausage, preserved meats, pickled cucumbers, rye bread and little hot pastries.

From Spain and the Middle East come tapas and meze. Traditionally served as snacks with drinks, they also make ideal appetisers. In Spain, tapas are served in bars. Sometimes free, they can come automatically with each drink, while in other bars you need to order them. Often salty (olives, anchovies or little rounds of spicy grilled chorizo), not only are they perfect with a chilled glass of sherry or a cold beer, but they also encourage the drinker to sip their libation. The range of tapas is enormous and varies from the classic spicy fried potatoes (patatas bravas) to wedges of tortilla, salads and wonderful fish and shellfish.

In contrast, meze are usually served in the home, as an array of snacks to offer guests. The word meze comes from the Persian "maz", meaning "taste" or "relish", and the tradition spreads from Turkey into Greece, Lebanon and throughout north Africa. Typically, meze range from olives or cubes of cheese to dips, such as taramasalata, tsatsiki and hummus, salads, such as tabbouleh, and more substantial falafel and little pastries.

Asia also produces an inspired array of snacks that are perfect for starting a meal. Japanese sushi appeals to the eye and palate, and the smaller portions are perfect for popping into your mouth as you chat over drinks. Similarly, Chinese dim sum are ideal to get the digestive juices flowing. Something of a Chinese tapas, traditionally dim sum are served in tea houses and one would no more consider going to a tea house without ordering a few of these little morsels than going to a tapas bar and not ordering a little something to accompany your drink. And then there are those classic street-foods – the snacks sold on street corners all over Asia – from Indian samosas and pakoras to Thai fishcakes and roasted cashews, Indonesian satay and Vietnamese salt-and-pepper squid.

equipment

You rarely need special equipment for preparing and cooking appetisers, other than the usual kitchen kit – a good, sharp knife and board, mixing bowls and spoons, measuring spoons, cups, jugs and scales, a baking sheet and wire rack, pans, food processor or blender and so on. Only a few appetisers, such as sushi, will require specialist equipment (such as a sushi mat for rolling up classic sushi rolls). However, serving is important because beautiful presentation has as much to do with making the mouth water as the aroma of the food.

serving bowls and platters
These are particularly important for canapés, cocktail snacks, and dips and dippers.
• Large, flat platters are perfect for canapés, tartlets, pizza squares and skewered foods.
• A large dish or shallow bowl big enough to hold a smaller bowl is perfect for serving dips and dippers together.
• Smaller bowls are ideal for olives, nuts and cocktail crackers.

individual plates and bowls
For appetisers enjoyed at the table, such as salads and tarts, placing them on individual plates adds a special style. A salad arranged on a small plate or in an individual bowl usually looks far more appealing than one served in a large dish, to be spooned out at the table. For tapas or meze, where several small items are served at once, you will need several small serving dishes as well as plates for guests to pile with the morsels on offer.

skewers, picks and sticks
These are essential, not only for satay or kebabs but also good for skewering "messy" or awkward foods, such as salt-and-pepper squid or marinated olives. There is a wide variety of skewers available, from the simplest bamboo type to metal skewers with decorative handles.

The simplest picks, sticks and spikes for selecting pieces of food are cocktail sticks or toothpicks, while decorative sticks transform simple ingredients into elegant appetizers.

napkins

Napkins are essential for cleaning sticky or greasy fingers, or for holding larger snacks that provide two or three mouthfuls before they are finished. A pizza square or golden chicken wing is so much easier to handle when you have a napkin to rest it on as you chat between mouthfuls. Paper napkins are entirely acceptable for appetisers served with drinks, but for a more formal course at the table you may prefer to go for linen.

debris dishes

Foods that leave guests clutching redundant olive stones, skewers or bones always have to be shadowed by strategically placed vessels for unwanted leftovers. These foods help get a party going and smooth the way for social chit-chat – so having guests wondering how to discard nibble-sticks without causing a terrible social faux pas is not ideal!

gorgeous garnishes

The garnish contributes visual appeal and it should also be aromatic and flavoursome. Fresh herbs are a great standby, whether sprinkled over soups, on canapés or meze. A single basil or rocket leaf, a sprinkling of black pepper or paprika, or a twist of lemon or cucumber can be the finishing touch that turns a lovely canapé into a simply stunning one. Snipped chives, a sprig of oregano or a fragrant leaf, a wafer-thin slice of cucumber or half a cherry tomato, a twist of smoked salmon or a blob of caviar can be prepared ahead and transferred to the food with minimum effort. In this way, you can top, drizzle or sprinkle in a matter of seconds and serve up appetisers that look utterly irresistible with that just-made appearance.

making perfect appetisers

There are a few tricks for producing perfect appetisers. The main one is choosing the right appetiser for the right occasion. Are you throwing an elegant dinner party where you want to impress your guests? Or is it a more casual affair when a laid-back, anything-goes style is more suitable? Have you invited an intrepid crowd who'll try anything once? Or is it a guest list of elderly relatives who would prefer to eat something they know and love, rather than try out something new and exotic? Or are you entertaining a crowd of ravenous teenagers who'll eat anything and everything in sight? Whoever you're entertaining, this book is packed with fun, delicious ideas that will suit any and every occasion.

For a fairly formal affair, dip into the chapters on mouthwatering salads and elegant starters. Each recipe tastes delicious, looks stunning and is guaranteed to impress even the most discerning diners. For a casual occasion, why not try simple dips, chips and batons – they're great with drinks, for a family meal, or for an informal party. For a taste of the exotic, nothing beats a plateful of meze or Asian-style snacks. Those with more conventional taste will find little more enjoyable than simple chips and dips, or a light salad of fresh leaves.

getting the timing right

Good timing is a key feature of the perfect appetiser. Who wants to slave away in the kitchen while their guests are having fun? Choose appetisers that suit you, the cook. If you're serving at the kitchen table, chatting while cooking can be fun, but if you're entertaining elsewhere, go for dishes that can be prepared ahead and assembled at the last minute.

Most dips can be stored in the fridge, with just a quick stir before serving, and skewers can be left to marinate until it is time to grill them. Salads can be prepared ahead and dressed before serving. Canapé toppings and bases can be assembled at the last minute.

It is also paramount to remember that an appetiser is just one course and that there is more to follow. So choosing an impressive, yet hassle-free, appetiser means you can

concentrate on getting the main course and dessert just right, knowing that the appetiser will keep everyone happy while you stay cool, calm and collected.

dressing up and dressing down

Perfect presentation is key. The great thing about presentation is that you can dress dishes up or down to suit the occasion. A big basket of chicken wings plonked on the table for the family to dig into is the ultimate relaxing, low-maintenance appetiser. Conversely, toss a bag of salad leaves with a simple dressing, arrange it on plates and nestle a few chicken wings on top, and an altogether more impressive appetiser evolves with minimum effort.

Many of the recipes in this book can be dressed up or down according to the occasion. Nestle three or four canapés on each plate with a few salad leaves, add a drizzle of dressing and suddenly you have an elegant starter rather than a pre-dinner nibble. Meze, tapas and Asian bites can all be treated in this way too. Simple salads with chicken satay accompanied by tiny pots of satay sauce provide an entirely different tone from a platter of satay with a hunky bowl of peanut sauce, passed around as everyone sips aperitifs or cocktails.

Meze, tapas or Asian snacks are also the perfect choice if you fancy an exotic feast of dishes from around the world. Why not start with a selection of meze before moving on to a main course of a Moroccan tagine with couscous and a simple dessert of rosewater ice cream? Alternatively, nibble on a few tapas tasters before serving a fabulous seafood paella, followed by the classic Spanish dessert crema catalana. Asian snacks, inspired by classic street food, are the ultimate in dress-up or dress-down appetisers – as good served with drinks and a simple dip as plated up with drizzled sauces and cucumber salad or relish.

Dips are fantastically versatile too. Choose any of the dips in this book, just dollop some on to squares of pumpernickel or mini blinis, sprinkle with fresh herbs and...voila! Suddenly you have a plate of stunning canapés, perfect for the most sophisticated of drinks parties.

The trick is to have fun. Use creative flair to transform your no-hassle, favourite savoury to suit any occasion.

instant appetisers

As well as working from recipes, there's a fabulous choice of instant appetisers to conjure up at a moment's notice and put you in the ultimate-host category with almost no effort!

quick dips

Supermarkets sell a range of fabulous ready-made dips, from fresh salsas to creamy classics and simple favourites, such as guacamole, taramasalata and hummus. Just buy a tub, scoop it into a bowl and serve with some dippers and your work is done.

If you want to make super-speedy dips of your own, go for a simple base, such as a good-quality mayonnaise, crème fraîche, sour cream or plain yogurt. Stir in chopped fresh herbs, lemon rind, a spoonful or two of pesto or a little crumbled blue cheese to make a simple dip. Other good additions include a splash or two of Tabasco sauce, finely chopped spring onion, capers, crushed anchovy or garlic.

easy dippers

Every dip needs tasty dippers. Bought savoury snacks can be good on their own or for dunking. Just open the bag when guests arrive, tip them into a bowl and serve. What could be simpler? Select artisan crisps in a great choice of interesting flavours – guests are sure to be impressed that you've searched out special snacks rather than the usual supermarket fare.

Other fuss-free dippers include fingers of pitta bread, either plain or lightly toasted. Crisp Italian breadsticks are another good choice for kids and adults alike. Tortilla chips and mini poppadoms are great for scooping, whether it's a Mexican-style salsa or a fragrant Indian relish; they're great for topping too. Depending on the occasion, turn them into bites with sophisticated toppings or simple munchies.

Raw vegetable sticks are ideal for dipping and dunking, and make a refreshing, healthy choice. Depending on the vegetables, these can take more or less time to prepare. Carrots should be topped, tailed and peeled, then cut into bite-size sticks. Cucumbers should be washed, seeded and cut into sticks. Peppers should be seeded, then sliced into sticks. Broccoli and cauliflower florets and cherry tomatoes are also good. As a rule, it is best not to prepare vegetable sticks too far ahead as they dry out. If you need to prepare them some time in advance, place them in a bowl and cover tightly with clear film, then store in the fridge until ready to serve.

minute munchies
There's a wide choice of nibbles to go with drinks to serve up in a moment. Olives or some marinated anchovies from the deli counter, a bag of honey-roasted nuts or a bowl of exotic cheese crackers are all you need. Buy a can of stuffed vine leaves, arrange them on a platter and simply squeeze lime juice over – delicious! Remember, it's all in the presentation.

shortcuts to canapés
Canapés are traditionally presented on some kind of bread base. Although you can make your own, there are plenty of shortcuts that look stunning and save time and hassle.
• Blinis are available from most larger supermarkets, ready to be heated quickly in the oven.
• Pumpernickel is another great choice. Cut it into squares or use a cookie cutter to cut it into bite-size rounds and add the topping of your choice. You can use this technique on toasted bread as well. The result looks stunning but takes no effort at all.
• Plain flour tortillas make another fuss-free 'base'. Smear them with a thin layer of filling, such as cream cheese, and add some smoked salmon. Then roll them up tightly and slice the roll using a sharp serrated knife to make a plateful of mini pinwheels. Alternatively, cut the tortillas in half or into quarters and roll the pieces into mini cones ready to hold the filling of your choice.

fuss-free ingredients

As well as tricks and tips for making instant appetisers, there are also a number of ingredients that can take all the hassle out of preparation, which is just what you need when there are two more courses to prepare!

• Char-grilled or roasted vegetables are available bottled in olive oil. These taste great and are a godsend for first courses. Wedges of char-grilled artichokes and twists of roasted pepper look great on canapés or tossed into salads. Look out for Italian antipasti too – the vegetables are often bottled in a flavoursome marinade that will really add a twist of flavour to a plain starter.

• Caper berries taste great and look more exotic than your average caper popped on top of a canapé or scattered on salad.

• Don't worry about cutting up your own crudités: buy a ready-prepared bag.

• To make polenta crostini, buy a block of ready-made polenta, then simply slice, brush with oil and grill or fry until crisp before topping.

• Chickpeas and other pulses are great for wholesome dips. Don't soak and boil for hours but buy canned instead, then drain them, throw them into the food processor with the chosen flavourings, blitz for a moment, and you've got a delicious dip!

• Ready-rolled pastry is another boon for the busy cook. Simply take it out of the packet, cut into the required shapes, add toppings and bake. What could be easier?

• Ready-made pizza bases, like ready-rolled pastry, are also a great time saver.

• Mini pitta breads can be turned into instant pizza: top with pizza sauce and cheese, and bake for 10 minutes until golden.

• Naan bread can be transformed into hearty pizza ovals, then cut into wedges for the hungry masses.

• For salads, buy ready-prepared leaves. There are lots of inspired mixtures and it is so much easier than trying to create your own mixture of many leaves. The average bag is the perfect size for four appetizers, just right for most of the recipes in this book.

chips & batons

These easy nibbles are crisp and satisfying – sure to please even the youngest party guest. Serve them on their own, buy a tub of ready made dip, or pair them with one of the delicious dips in the next chapter. What could be simpler?

walnut & sun-dried tomato biscotti

see variations page 38

Based on the classic twice-baked Italian biscuit, these savoury bites are a great alternative to crisps. Their long, thin shape also makes them perfect for dunking into dips.

55 g/2 oz butter at room temperature
2 eggs, lightly beaten
115 g/4 oz self-raising flour
55 g/2 oz polenta

55 g/2 oz (about 10) sun-dried tomatoes in oil, drained and chopped
55 g/2 oz walnuts, chopped

Preheat the oven to 180°C/350°F/Gas Mark 4 and lightly grease and flour two baking sheets.

Beat the butter until smooth and creamy, then gradually beat in the eggs a little at a time. Sift the flour and polenta over the butter mixture and fold in using a metal spoon. Then stir in the sun-dried tomatoes and walnuts.

Divide the mixture between the baking sheets, shaping two flat loaves about 18 x 7.5 cm/7 x 3 in. Bake the loaves for about 20 minutes until pale golden, then transfer them to a board.

Using a serrated knife, cut into 1 cm/^{1}/$_2$ in slices. Arrange the slices on the baking sheets and cook for 10 minutes, until crisp and golden. Transfer to a wire rack to cool.

Makes about 24

parmesan tuiles

see variations page 39

These melt-in-the-mouth wafers are ridiculously easy to make and great for munching or dunking in a smooth dip. They can be stored in an airtight container for several days.

115 g/4 oz Parmesan cheese, grated

Preheat the oven to 200°C/400°F/Gas Mark 6. Line two baking sheets with non-stick baking parchment, right up to the edge.

Spoon small mounds of cheese spaced well apart on the baking sheets and flatten them into rounds using the back of the spoon.

Bake the Parmesan for about 5 minutes, until golden. Leave the Parmesan tuiles on the baking sheets for a minute or so, to firm up. Use a palette knife to remove them carefully from the paper and curl them over a rolling pin until set. Allow the tuiles to cool completely on a wire rack.

Makes about 10

mozzarella &
basil quesadilla wedges

see variations page 40

Serve these melting Mexican wedges on their own or pair them with a tangy, zingy salsa for dipping.

Olive oil, for brushing
2 soft flour tortillas
150 g/5 oz mozzarella cheese, thinly sliced

Dried chilli flakes, for sprinkling
Handful of fresh basil leaves

Brush a large, non-stick frying pan with olive oil and heat it. Lay 1 tortilla in the pan and arrange the cheese on top. Sprinkle over a good pinch or two of chilli flakes and the basil leaves. Lay the second tortilla on top.

Cook for 1 to 2 minutes, until the tortilla is crisp and golden underneath. Then carefully flip it over and cook for a further 1 to 2 minutes, until crisp and golden on the second side.

Slide the tortilla out onto a board, cut it into 12 wedges and serve immediately.

Makes 12

poppy seed grissini

see variations page 41

These crunchy Italian breadsticks are delicious eaten as they are or served with a tangy dip. If you're feeling adventurous, try making a few different varieties to serve together.

200 g/7 oz strong white bread flour
1 tsp easy blend dried yeast
$1/2$ tsp salt

1 tbsp olive oil
120 ml/4 fl oz warm water
2 tsp poppy seeds

Combine the flour, yeast and salt in a large bowl and make a well in the middle. Pour in the oil and water and mix to a soft dough.

Turn out the dough on to a lightly floured surface and knead it for 5 to 10 minutes until it is smooth and elastic. Place the dough in a large, clean oiled bowl, cover with oiled clear film and leave to rise in a warm place for about 1 hour or until doubled in size.

Preheat the oven to 200°C/400°F/Gas Mark 6 and lightly grease two baking sheets. Roll out the dough on a lightly floured surface into a 20 x 30-cm/6 x 12-in rectangle and cut into 1 cm/$1/2$ in wide strips. Lightly roll the strips and arrange on the baking sheet, spacing them well apart.

Brush the grissini with water, sprinkle with poppy seeds and bake for 10 to 12 minutes until golden. Transfer to a wire rack to cool.

Makes about 24

herbed garlic pitta toasts

see variations page 42

Serve these crispy, crunchy fingers of pitta on their own or with a creamy dip. You can use white or wholemeal pitta breads.

2 tbsp olive oil
1 garlic clove, crushed
Ground black pepper

2 pitta breads
1 tbsp chopped fresh parsley

In a small bowl, combine the oil and garlic and season with black pepper. Preheat the grill.

Cut the pitta breads in half horizontally, then carefully split them open. Slice each piece into three fingers. Arrange the pitta fingers on the grill rack and toast on one side for 1 to 2 minutes until crisp and golden.

Turn the pitta fingers, drizzle with the garlic oil and grill for a further minute or so until crisp and golden. Sprinkle with parsley and serve immediately.

Serves 4

simple rice noodle crisps

see variations page 43

These lacy rice noodle pancakes make a stunning pre-dinner snack – perfect for whetting the appetite before an Asian-style meal. Serve them solo or with sweet chilli sauce for dipping.

115 g/4 oz rice vermicelli
1 red chilli, seeded and finely chopped
1 tsp ground cumin

1 shallot, finely chopped
Salt
Vegetable oil, for deep-frying

Break the noodles into a large heatproof bowl and pour over boiling water to cover. Leave to stand for about 5 minutes, until softened.

Drain the noodles well and return them to the bowl. Sprinkle the chilli, cumin and shallot over the noodles, season with salt and toss together.

Heat about 5 cm/2 in oil to 190°C/375°F in a wok, or until a cube of bread turns golden in about 1 minute.

Working in batches, drop tablespoonfuls of the noodles into the wok, pressing them flat using the back of a slotted spoon. Cook for about 2 minutes until crisp and golden, then lift out and drain on kitchen paper. Serve immediately.

Makes about 24

chilli cheese straws

see variations page 44

Choose a really good, strongly flavoured cheese for these crisp little twists. They have a wonderful bite of chilli and are incredibly more-ish.

115 g/4 oz plain flour
85 g/3 oz butter, chilled and diced
85 g/3 oz mature Cheddar cheese, grated
$1/2$ tsp dried chilli flakes

1 tsp Worcestershire sauce
Paprika, for sprinkling (optional)

Process the flour and butter in a food processor until the mixture resembles fine breadcrumbs. Add the cheese, chilli and Worcestershire sauce and process to a soft dough.

Press the dough into a ball, wrap it in clear film and chill for about 15 minutes, until it has firmed up slightly. Preheat the oven to 170°C/325°C/Gas Mark 3.

Roll out the dough on a lightly floured surface to about 3 mm/$1/4$ in thick, then cut it into strips measuring about 1.5 cm/$3/4$ in wide and 8 cm/$31/2$ in long. Twist the strips and lay them on a baking sheet.

Bake the twists for 10–15 minutes, until crisp and golden. Transfer them to a wire rack to cool. Sprinkle with paprika, if liked, before serving.

Makes about 30

anchovy crackers

see variations page 45

These peppery, salty bites are perfect with pre-dinner drinks. They are intriguingly delicious and difficult to resist.

55 g/2 oz plain flour
55 g/2 oz butter, chilled and diced
28 g/1 oz freshly grated Parmesan cheese

4 anchovy fillets in oil, drained
$^1/_4$ to $^1/_2$ tsp ground black pepper

Process the flour, butter, Parmesan, anchovies and pepper in a food processor until the mixture comes together into a soft dough. Press the dough into a ball, wrap it in clear film and chill for about 15 minutes, until it has firmed up slightly.

Meanwhile, preheat the oven to 200°F/400°C/Gas Mark 6. Lightly grease two baking sheets.

Roll out the dough on a lightly floured surface to about 3 mm/$^1/_4$ in thick and cut into rounds using a 3-cm/1$^1/_4$-in cookie cutter. Press the dough trimmings together and re-roll to make more rounds.

Arrange the rounds on the baking sheets and bake for about 6 minutes, until golden. Transfer the crackers to a wire rack to cool.

Makes about 40

beetroot crisps

see variations page 46

These colourful crisps made from wafer thin slices of beetroot are easy to make and are great with drinks. Serve them on their own or with a little bowl of creamy dip.

1–2 beetroots
Sunflower oil, for deep-frying

Coarse sea salt, for sprinkling

Trim and peel the beetroot, then use a mandolin or vegetable peeler to slice them into thin shavings. Rinse well, then pat dry on kitchen paper.

Pour sunflower oil into a pan to fill it by about one-third and heat to 190°C/375°F, or until a cube of bread turns golden in about 1 minute.

Working in batches, deep-fry the beetroot slices for about 1 minute, until crisp. Lift the crisps out of the oil using a slotted spoon and drain them on a wire rack covered with several layers of kitchen paper. Sprinkle with salt and serve immediately.

Serves 4

tortilla chips

see variations page 47

Serve these crunchy golden chips on their own or Mexican-style with a spicy salsa or creamy guacamole.

2 soft flour tortillas
Vegetable oil, for deep-frying

Coarse sea salt, for sprinkling

Cut each tortilla into eight wedges. Pour oil into a deep frying pan until it is two-thirds full and heat to about 190°/375°F, or until a cube of bread turns golden in about 1 minute.

Working in batches, add the tortilla wedges to the oil and fry for about 2 minutes, until golden. Remove from the oil using a slotted spoon and drain on kitchen paper. Sprinkle with salt and serve.

Serves 4

variations

walnut & sun-dried tomato biscotti

see base recipe page 19

walnut & cranberry biscotti
Prepare the basic recipe, adding 50 g/2 oz dried cranberries in place of the sun-dried tomatoes.

spicy sun-dried tomato & walnut biscotti
Prepare the basic recipe, adding $1/2$ teaspoon crushed dried chilli flakes with the tomatoes and walnuts.

pecan & olive biscotti
Prepare the basic recipe, using roughly chopped pitted olives in place of the sun-dried tomatoes, and pecan nuts in place of the walnuts.

almond, chilli & date biscotti
Prepare the basic recipe, using almonds in place of the walnuts, and omitting the sun-dried tomatoes. Add $1/2$ teaspoon dried chilli flakes and 50 g/2 oz chopped pitted dried dates after folding in the flour.

parmesan tuiles

see base recipe page 21

fennel & parmesan tuiles
Sprinkle about $1/8$ teaspoon fennel seeds over the Parmesan before baking.

spicy cumin tuiles
Sprinkle a pinch or two of dried chilli flakes and a pinch or two of cumin seeds over the Parmesan before baking.

parmesan tuiles with thyme
Sprinkle about $1/8$ teaspoon fresh thyme leaves over the Parmesan before baking.

parmesan tuiles with sage
Sprinkle about $1/8$ teaspoon chopped fresh sage over the Parmesan before baking.

variations

mozzarella & basil quesadilla wedges

see base recipe page 22

hot jalepeno quesadilla wedges
Prepare the basic quesadilla recipe, using 2 tablespoons sliced bottled jalepenos in place of the dried chilli and basil leaves.

mozzarella & spinach quesadilla wedges
Prepare the basic quesadilla recipe, using a handful of baby spinach leaves in place of the basil leaves.

mozzarella & roast pepper quesadilla wedges
Prepare the basic quesadilla recipe, using 2 sliced bottled roasted peppers in place of the basil leaves.

mozzarella with roast pepper, basil and chilli quesadilla wedges
Prepare the basic quesadilla recipe, adding 2 sliced bottled roasted peppers with the basil and chilli.

mozzarella & sun-dried tomato quesadilla wedges
Slice 4 drained sun-dried tomatoes in olive oil. Prepare the basic quesadilla recipe, sprinkling over the sun-dried tomatoes in place of the basil leaves.

poppy seed grissini

see base recipe page 25

chunky breadstick twists
Prepare and roll out the basic dough, but cut it into 2 cm/³/₄ in wide strips.
Gently twist each strip and lay it on the baking sheet. Bake for about
17 minutes.

sesame seed grissini
Prepare the basic grisini recipe, using sesame seeds in place of the
poppy seeds.

parmesan grissini
Prepare the basic grisini recipe, using about 2 tablespoons freshly grated
Parmesan cheese in place of the poppy seeds.

fennel seed grissini
Prepare the basic grisini recipe, using fennel seeds in place of the
poppy seeds.

variations

herbed garlic pitta toasts

see base recipe page 26

garlic & lemon pitta wedges
Prepare the basic recipe, adding 1 teaspoon grated lemon rind to the olive oil mixture.

herbed pitta wedges
Prepare the basic recipe, omitting the garlic and sprinkling a mixture of chopped fresh chives, parsley and mint over the toasts.

spicy herb pitta wedges
Prepare the basic recipe, adding 1 seeded, finely chopped fresh red chilli to the olive oil in place of the garlic.

garlic, herb & chilli pitta wedges
Prepare the basic recipe, adding 1 seeded, finely chopped red chilli to the olive oil mixture.

simple rice noodle crisps

see base recipe page 29

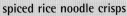

spiced rice noodle crisps
Prepare the basic recipe, adding 1 teaspoon ground coriander to the
noodle mixture.

rice noodle crisps with fennel
Prepare the basic recipe, adding $1/2$ teaspoon fennel seeds to the
noodle mixture.

rice noodle crisps with cardamom
Prepare the basic recipe, adding $1/2$ teaspoon crushed cardamom seeds to
the noodle mixture.

rice noodle crisps with garlic and ginger
Prepare the basic recipe, adding 1 crushed garlic clove and 1 teaspoon
grated fresh root ginger to the noodle mixture.

variations

chilli cheese straws

see base recipe page 30

cheese straws
Prepare the basic recipe, omitting the chilli. Lay the strips on baking sheets without twisting them.

blue cheese straws
Prepare the basic recipe, using crumbled blue cheese in place of the grated Cheddar. Omit the chilli and paprika.

herb cheese straws
Prepare the basic recipe, adding 1 teaspoon chopped fresh sage leaves in place of the crushed chilli.

garlicky cheese straws
Prepare the basic recipe, adding 1 crushed garlic clove.

variations

anchovy crackers

see base recipe page 33

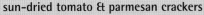

sun-dried tomato & parmesan crackers
Prepare the basic recipe, using 6 chopped sun-dried tomatoes in place of
the anchovies.

anchovy & parmesan wedges
Prepare the basic recipe, chill and roll out. Instead of using a cookie cutter,
cut the dough into triangles, then bake as before.

spicy anchovy crackers
Prepare the basic recipe, adding $1/4$ teaspoon dried chilli flakes in place of
the black pepper.

herb & anchovy crackers
Prepare the basic recipe, adding 1 teaspoon fresh thyme leaves to the
ingredients before processing.

variations

beetroot crisps

see base recipe page 34

parsnip crisps
Use 1 to 2 parsnips in place of the beetroot to make sweet, golden crisps.

sweet potato crisps
Use 1 sweet potato in place of the beetroot to make slightly sweet, golden-orange crisps.

pumpkin crisps
To make rich, orange-coloured crisps, use a wedge of pumpkin in place of the beetroot.

mixed vegetable crisps
Make multi-coloured crisps by using a mixture of root vegetables, such as beetroot, sweet potato, potato and pumpkin.

variations

tortilla chips

see base recipe page 36

smoky tortilla chips
Prepare the basic recipe and dust the tortilla chips with smoked paprika just
before serving.

tortilla chips with lime
Prepare the basic recipe and dust the tortilla chips with the finely grated
zest of $1/2$ lime just before serving.

curried tortilla chips
Prepare the basic recipe and dust the tortilla chips with garam masala just
before serving.

fiery tortilla chips
Prepare the basic recipe and dust the tortilla chips with cayenne pepper just
before serving.

dips & salsas

Nothing goes better with a salty crisp than a
bowlful of spicy salsa or creamy dip. Rich and
smooth, fresh and zesty, hot and spicy, or cool and
creamy – the recipes in his chapter are perfect for
laid-back snacking.

creamy artichoke dip

see variations page 65

Serve this smooth, mild and creamy dip with plain tortilla chips or breadsticks. This makes the perfect choice for those who want a reduced-fat dip.

14 oz/400 g can artichoke hearts, drained
1 garlic clove, crushed
1 tbsp extra virgin olive oil
$1/4$ tsp ground cumin

$1/4$ tsp grated lemon rind
Salt and ground black pepper
1 tbsp chopped fresh parsley

Put the artichokes, garlic, oil, cumin and lemon rind in a food processor. Add seasoning and blend to make a smooth purée.

Check the seasoning and stir in the parsley. Scrape the dip into a bowl and serve.

Serves 4

fresh tomato & red onion salsa

see variations page 66

Fresh and tangy, this peppery tomato salsa is simple to prepare and it makes a great informal, summery appetizer. For a Mexican feel, serve tortilla chips or quesadilla wedges with the dip.

3 tomatoes, seeded and finely chopped
1 red onion, quartered and finely sliced
1 green chilli, seeded and finely chopped
3 good pinches of ground cumin

1 tsp red wine vinegar
1 tbsp olive oil
Salt
2 tbsp chopped fresh coriander leaves

Put the tomatoes, onion, chilli, cumin, vinegar and oil in a bowl. Season with salt and toss to combine. Add the coriander and toss again. Turn the salsa into a bowl and serve.

Serves 4

avocado salsa

see variations page 67

This classic salsa can be served as a dip with chunky dippers, such as tortilla chips or pitta wedges, for scooping.

2 avocados, peeled, stoned and finely chopped
2 tomatoes, seeded and finely chopped
1 red chilli, seeded and finely chopped
2 spring onions, finely sliced

Handful of fresh coriander leaves, chopped
Salt
1 lime

Put the avocados, tomatoes, chilli, spring onions and coriander in a bowl. Season with salt and toss to combine.

Squeeze lime juice over to taste and toss the mixture again. Transfer the salsa to a bowl and serve within 2 hours. Avocado discolours if it is left to stand for too long – this can be minimized by covering the surface of the salsa directly with plastic wrap to keep the air out and chilling the salsa.

Serves 4

minty cucumber & yogurt dip

see variations page 68

This refreshing dip based on the classic Greek tzatziki, makes a perfect light, informal appetizer. Serve it with crisps for scooping.

1/2 large cucumber
235 ml/8 fl oz Greek yogurt
1 garlic clove, crushed

2 tbsp chopped fresh mint
Salt

Peel the cucumber, cut it in half lengthways and scrape out the seeds. Then grate the cucumber and place it in a sieve. Press out as much liquid as possible.

Place the cucumber in a bowl and mix in the yogurt, garlic and mint. Season to taste with salt. Transfer to a bowl and chill until ready to serve.

Serves 4

fiery pumpkin dip

see variations page 69

This glorious orange dip offers a rich combination of sweet, spicy, fiery and sour flavours. But be warned – once you start dipping, it's hard to stop.

600 g/1 lb 5 oz butternut squash or pumpkin,
    seeded, peeled and cut into chunks
2 tbsp olive oil
Salt and ground black pepper

1 garlic clove, crushed
1 tsp grated fresh root ginger
1 red chilli, seeded and finely chopped
Juice of 1/2 lime

Preheat the oven to 200°C/400°F/Gas Mark 6. Put the squash or pumpkin in a baking dish, drizzle over 1 tbsp of the oil and season with salt and pepper. Roast for about 20 minutes, tossing once or twice during cooking, until tender.

Tip the squash into a food processor and add the garlic, ginger, chilli and remaining oil. Process until smooth, then briefly pulse in the lime juice and check the seasoning.

Scrape the dip into a bowl and serve hot, warm or cold. (It will thicken on cooling, so give it a good stir before serving.)

Serves 4

courgette & caper dip

see variations page 70

This light and tangy dip makes a healthy choice if you want a smooth, creamy dip without the calories. Serve it hot or cold with crackers or pitta toasts.

3 courgettes, sliced
$1/2$ garlic clove, crushed
2 tsp capers, rinsed
Good pinch of dried chilli flakes

2 tbsp olive oil
Salt
$1/4$ lemon

Cook the courgettes in a steamer over a pan of boiling water for about 5 minutes, until they are tender.

Tip the courgettes into a food processor and add the garlic, capers, chilli and olive oil. Process to a smooth purée. Check the seasoning and add lemon juice to taste.

Transfer the dip to a bowl and serve hot. Alternatively leave to cool before serving.

Serves 4

roast red pepper & walnut dip

see variations page 71

Richly flavoured with walnuts and smoky peppers, served with chilled white wine, this is the perfect dip for summer barbecues.

2 large red peppers
55 g/2 oz walnuts
$^1/_2$ tsp paprika
$^1/_4$ tsp ground ginger
Good pinch of cayenne pepper

1 garlic clove, crushed
2 tbsp olive oil
Salt
2 tsp lemon juice
2 tsp chopped fresh mint

Preheat the oven to 230°C/450°F/Gas Mark 8. Place the peppers on a baking sheet and roast them for about 30 minutes, until blackened. Put the peppers in a bowl, cover with clear film and leave to stand for about 20 minutes, until they are cool enough to handle and the skins have loosened.

Peel and seed the peppers, then put the flesh in a food processor with the walnuts, paprika, ginger, cayenne pepper, garlic and oil. Season with salt and process to a smooth purée.

Transfer the dip to a bowl, stir in lemon juice to taste and adjust the seasoning. Leave to cool, then stir in the mint and serve at room temperature.

Serves 4

flageolet bean & pesto dip

see variations page 72

Whet the appetite by serving this creamy bean dip with fresh, crunchy vegetable crudités: carrot sticks, cherry tomatoes and strips of red pepper go particularly well.

400 g/14 oz can flageolet beans, drained and
   rinsed
1 garlic clove, crushed
$1/4$ tsp dried chilli flakes

$3^1/_2$ tbsp green pesto
2 tbsp olive oil
1 tsp lemon juice

Process the beans, garlic, chilli, pesto and oil in a food processor to make a smooth purée.

Add lemon juice to taste and process briefly, then spoon the dip into a bowl and serve.

Serves 4

beetroot & ginger dip

see variations page 73

Shocking pink and rich with garlic and ginger, this stunning dip is guaranteed to arouse the appetite.

250 g/9 oz cooked beetroot, roughly chopped
1 garlic clove, crushed
2 tsp ground coriander
$1/2$ tsp ground ginger

Salt and ground black pepper
175 ml/6 fl oz Greek yogurt
1 tsp chopped fresh mint

Put the beetroot, garlic, coriander and ginger in a food processor and season with salt and pepper. Process to a smooth purée.

Add the yogurt and process briefly to combine it with the other ingredients. Check the seasoning, then scrape the dip into a bowl, sprinkle the mint over and serve.

Serves 4

creamy artichoke dip

see base recipe page 49

artichoke & chive dip
Prepare the basic recipe, adding snipped chives in place of the parsley.

artichoke dip with sweet paprika
Prepare the basic recipe, adding a good pinch of paprika.

artichoke dip with pesto
Prepare the basic dip, adding 1 to 2 tablespoons green pesto in place of the lemon rind and cumin.

extra-creamy artichoke dip
Prepare the basic recipe, adding 2 tablespoons crème fraîche with the parsley.

variations

fresh tomato & red onion salsa

see base recipe page 51

tomato & red onion salsa with basil
Prepare the basic recipe, replacing the fresh coriander leaves with a small handful of torn fresh basil leaves.

tomato, pepper & red onion salsa
Preheat the oven to 230°C/450°F/Gas Mark 8. Place 1 red pepper on a baking sheet and bake for about 30 minutes, until blackened. Put the pepper in a bowl, cover with clear film and leave to stand for about 10 minutes. Peel and seed the pepper, then finely chop the flesh. Prepare the basic recipe, adding the chopped red pepper with the tomatoes.

tomato & mango salsa
Prepare the basic recipe, adding $1/2$ peeled, stoned and diced mango.

tomato & spring onion salsa
Prepare the basic recipe, adding a bunch of finely sliced spring onions in place of the red onion.

mild tomato & red onion salsa
Prepare the basic salsa, omitting the green chilli. Add a good grinding of black pepper or a pinch of paprika instead.

variations

avocado salsa

see base recipe page 52

guacamole
Using the ingredients in the basic recipe, first mash the avocados to make a smooth paste, then fold in the other ingredients and season with salt and lime juice to taste.

avocado & kiwi salsa
Prepare the basic recipe, adding 1 peeled, finely chopped kiwi fruit with the coriander.

avocado & mango salsa
Prepare the basic recipe, adding $1/2$ peeled, stoned and finely chopped mango with the avocado.

mild avocado salsa
Prepare the basic recipe, omitting the chilli. Add a good grinding of black pepper and a pinch of ground cumin instead.

avocado & red pepper salsa
Prepare the basic recipe, adding $1/2$ seeded and finely chopped red pepper with the avocado.

variations

minty cucumber & yogurt dip

see base recipe page 55

garlicky yogurt dip
Prepare the basic recipe, adding an extra clove of crushed garlic.

spicy cucumber & yogurt dip
Prepare the basic recipe, adding 1 seeded and finely chopped green chilli.

cucumber, spring onion & yogurt dip
Prepare the basic recipe, adding 3 finely sliced spring onions.

herb, cucumber & mint dip
Prepare the basic recipe, adding 1 tablespoon snipped fresh chives and
1 tablespoon chopped fresh coriander leaves with the mint.

variations

fiery pumpkin dip

see base recipe page 56

chunky pumpkin dip
Instead of using a food processor, coarsely mash the squash or pumpkin by hand and stir in the other ingredients to produce a chunkier dip.

spiced pumpkin dip
Prepare the basic recipe, omitting the chilli. Add 1 teaspoon ground cumin and 1 teaspoon ground coriander with the garlic and ginger.

curried pumpkin dip
Prepare the basic recipe, adding 1 teaspoon medium curry paste to the cooked pumpkin and the juice of $1/2$ to 1 lemon instead of the lime juice.

spicy pumpkin dip with harissa
Prepare the basic recipe, omitting the chilli and adding 1 teaspoon harissa paste and 1 teaspoon ground cumin instead.

variations

courgette & caper dip

see base recipe page 59

lemon courgette dip
Prepare the basic recipe, adding $1/2$ teaspoon grated lemon rind with the lemon juice.

creamy courgette dip
Prepare the basic recipe, omitting the chilli and adding 3 tablespoons crème fraîche with the lemon juice.

courgette & dill dip
Prepare the basic dip, adding 1 tablespoon chopped fresh dill and 2 tablespoons crème fraîche with the lemon juice.

minted courgette dip
Prepare the basic recipe, adding 1 teaspoon chopped fresh mint to the food processor. Sprinkle with extra chopped fresh mint before serving.

courgette, caper & parsley dip
Prepare the basic recipe, adding 2 tablespoons chopped fresh parsley to the food processor. Sprinkle with more parsley when serving.

roast red pepper & walnut dip

see base recipe page 60

creamy roast pepper dip
Prepare the basic recipe, then stir in 3 tablespoons crème fraîche when the dip has cooled.

roast pepper & cashew nut dip
Prepare the basic recipe using cashew nuts in place of the walnuts.

roast red pepper & walnut dip with basil
Prepare the basic recipe, adding a small handful of fresh basil leaves to the food processor, and omitting the mint.

roast red pepper with pine nuts & basil
Prepare the basic recipe, using pine nuts in place of the walnuts and adding a small handful of fresh basil leaves instead of the mint.

variations

flageolet bean & pesto dip

see base recipe page 63

cannelini bean & red pesto dip
Prepare the basic recipe using cannelini beans in place of the flageolet beans, and red pesto in place of green pesto.

flageolet bean & courgette dip
Slice 1 courgette and steam the slices over boiling water for about 5 minutes, until tender. Prepare the basic recipe, adding the steamed courgette with the beans, and process to make a smooth dip.

flageolet bean & roast pepper dip
Prepare the basic recipe, adding 2 drained bottled roasted peppers to the food processor with the beans.

extra-creamy flageolet bean dip
Prepare the basic dip and stir in 2 tablespoons crème fraîche with the lemon juice.

variations

beetroot & ginger dip

see base recipe page 64

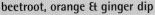

beetroot, orange & ginger dip
Prepare the basic recipe, adding the grated rind of $1/2$ orange with
the yogurt.

spicy beetroot & ginger dip
Prepare the basic recipe, adding 1 teaspoon harissa paste or 1 teaspoon
paprika and a good pinch of cayenne pepper.

beetroot & ginger dip with chives
Prepare the basic recipe, and sprinkle with snipped chives in place of the
mint before serving.

beetroot & ginger dip with coriander
Prepare the basic dip, and sprinkle with chopped fresh coriander leaves in
place of the mint.

mini mouthfuls

Good things come in small packages, and these tiny snacks pack a hearty punch. From nuts to cheese, olives to mushrooms, no-one will be able to resist taking just one more of these tiny morsels – each one designed to make the mouth water.

marinated olives

see variations page 91

A simple bowl of fragrant, marinated olives is all you need to whet the appetite. They can be simple or sophisticated and are utterly irresistible every time.

2 garlic cloves, sliced
Good pinch of dried chilli flakes
1 tsp chopped fresh rosemary
1 tbsp chopped flat-leaf parsley

1 tbsp wine vinegar
2 tbsp olive oil
250 g/9 oz black or green olives

Whisk together the garlic, dried chilli, rosemary, parsley, vinegar and olive oil in a bowl large enough to hold the olives.

Add the olives to the marinade and toss to coat them thoroughly. Cover and chill for at least 4 hours before serving. The olives will keep well for 3 to 4 days in the refrigerator.

Serves 4

quail's eggs with
black olive tapenade

see variations page 92

Tiny quail's eggs are delicious dipped into the salty, pungent, black olive and anchovy paste known as tapenade. The perfect bite-size morsel with pre-dinner drinks.

12 quail's eggs
200 g/7 oz pitted black olives
2 garlic cloves, crushed
3 anchovy fillets

2 tsp capers, rinsed and drained
1–2 tbsp olive oil
Squeeze of lemon juice
Black pepper

Bring a pan of water to the boil. Gently add the quail's eggs and boil for 4 minutes. Drain the eggs, return them to the pan and cover with cold water. Leave to cool.

For the tapenade, put the olives, garlic, anchovies, capers and olive oil in a food processor. Season with black pepper and process to a smooth purée. Add lemon juice to taste. Scrape the tapenade into a small dish and place on a serving platter.

Half-shell the eggs, leaving a neat base of shell to hold, arrange them around the dish of tapenade and serve.

Serves 4

smoky spiced almonds

see variations page 93

Serve these crisp, smoky nuts the Spanish way, with a glass of chilled sherry or a long cool glass of beer.

1 tsp olive oil
200 g/7 oz blanched almonds

Coarse sea salt
1/4 tsp smoked paprika

Heat the olive oil in a non-stick pan, then add the almonds and toss over the heat for about 5 minutes until golden.

Use a slotted spoon to transfer the nuts to a bowl, leaving as much oil in the pan as possible. Sprinkle generously with coarse sea salt and the paprika, and toss the nuts to coat them in the seasoning. Leave to cool then transfer to a serving dish.

Serves 4 to 8

garlic mushrooms

see variations page 94

Serve these juicy, flavoursome mushrooms with toothpicks so your guests can pick them up and pop them in their mouths without getting their fingers sticky.

1¹/₂ tbsp olive oil
2 garlic cloves, crushed
200 g/7 oz button mushrooms
2 tbsp white wine

1 tsp tomato purée
¹/₂ tsp fresh thyme leaves, plus extra for
  garnishing
Salt and ground black pepper

Pour the olive oil into a frying pan. Gently fry the garlic in the oil for about 1 minute, then add the mushrooms and toss to coat in the oil.

Stir the wine and tomato purée together and pour over the mushrooms, then add the thyme and season with salt and pepper. Cook gently for 15 to 20 minutes, stirring occasionally, until most of the juices have evaporated and the mushrooms are juicy and glossy but not wet.

Transfer to a serving dish. Serve hot, warm or at room temperature, sprinkled with a few fresh thyme leaves.

Serves 4

spicy prawn skewers

see variations page 95

With a fresh, zesty flavour, these simple skewers make a great informal appetizer to serve with drinks. To make a more formal first course, serve the skewers on lightly dressed salad leaves.

1 tsp grated fresh root ginger
1 garlic clove, crushed
Grated rind of $^1/_2$ lime and juice of 1 lime
16–20 raw tiger prawns, peeled and deveined

Salt and ground black pepper
Chopped fresh mint, for sprinkling
Sweet chilli sauce, for dipping

Soak twelve short bamboo skewers in water for 10 to 20 minutes. Mix the ginger, garlic and lime rind and juice in a large bowl and season with salt and pepper. Add the prawns, toss to coat them in the seasonings and cover. Chill for about 5 minutes.

Preheat the grill, or heat a ridged griddle pan. Thread a prawn lengthways on to the end of each skewer. Arrange the prawns on the grill pan or griddle and cook for about 1 minute on each side, until pink and cooked through.

Transfer the cooked prawns to a platter and sprinkle with mint. Serve immediately with chilli sauce for dipping.

Serves 4

prosciutto-wrapped asparagus with lemon mayo

see variations page 96

These sophisticated bites make an irresistible nibble with aperitifs or as a more formal appetizer. You can prepare everything ahead, then simply pop them in the oven when your guests arrive.

120 ml/4 fl oz mayonnaise
Grated rind of 1 lemon
1 tbsp lemon juice
$1/2$ tbsp snipped fresh chives

200 g/7 oz asparagus tips
8 wafer-thin slices prosciutto, cut into strips
Olive oil, for drizzling
Ground black pepper

Preheat the oven to 190°C/375°F/Gas Mark 5. Combine the mayonnaise, lemon rind, juice and dill in a serving dish. Cover and place in the refrigerator.

Wrap each asparagus tip in a strip of prosciutto, arrange on a baking sheet and drizzle with the oil. Grind a little black pepper over and roast for 6 to 7 minutes, until tender.

Transfer the prosciutto-wrapped asparagus to a platter and serve with the lemon mayonnaise.

Serves 4

bocconcini with mint & chilli

see variations page 97

You can usually buy bocconcini – the bite-size balls of mozzarella – in most good cheese shops, larger supermarkets and delis. Alternatively, use regular mozzarella and cut it into bite-size pieces.

250 g/9 oz bocconcini mozzarella
1/4 tsp dried chilli flakes

1 tsp chopped fresh mint
1 1/2 tbsp extra virgin olive oil

Drain the bocconcini and place in a bowl. Sprinkle with the chilli and mint and drizzle with the oil. Toss to coat each ball well in the herbs, spices and oil.

Cover and leave to marinate in the refrigerator for at least 1 hour. Allow the cheese to return to room temperature before serving.

Serves 4

tomato & mozzarella skewers

see variations page 98

These pretty red and white skewers take no time to put together. The salsa's also quick to whizz up and you can make it in advance to save time when guests arrive.

2 handfuls fresh basil leaves
2 tsp capers, rinsed
$1/2$ tsp Dijon mustard
$1^1/2$ tsp balsamic vinegar

4 tbsp olive oil
115 g/4 oz mozzarella, drained
20 cherry tomatoes
Ground black pepper

To make the salsa, put the basil leaves, capers, mustard, vinegar and olive oil in a small blender, season with black pepper and process until smooth. Transfer the mixture to a serving bowl, cover and chill, if preparing ahead, until ready to serve.

Cut the mozarella into 20 bite-size cubes. Thread 20 cocktail skewers each with a piece of cheese and a cherry tomato. Arrange the skewers on a serving platter with the salsa verde for dipping.

Makes 20

feta & watermelon spikes

see variations page 99

These refreshing, salty, piquant little mouthfuls are perfect for whetting the appetite before a meal on a balmy, hot summer afternoon or evening.

Small wedge of watermelon (about 450 g/1 lb), chilled
200 g/7 oz feta cheese

A little lime juice
Ground black pepper

Peel the watermelon and remove the black seeds, then cut the flesh into 24 bite-size chunks. Cut the cheese into 24 bite-size cubes.

Skewer a cube of cheese and a cube of watermelon on each of 24 cocktail sticks. Squeeze a little lime juice over the skewers, grind over some black pepper and serve.

Makes 24

variations

marinated olives

see base recipe page 75

red-hot marinated olives
Prepare the basic recipe, omitting the crushed dried chilli and adding
1 sliced fresh red chilli instead. Remove the seeds from the chilli for a
slightly milder result.

fragrant marinated olives
Prepare the basic recipe, adding $1/2$ teaspoon crushed toasted coriander
seeds.

marinated olives with oregano
Prepare the basic recipe, omitting the rosemary and adding 1 teaspoon
bruised oregano leaves instead.

cumin-spiced olives
Prepare the basic recipe, omitting the rosemary and adding $1/2$ teaspoon
ground cumin instead.

marinated olives with fresh mint
Prepare the basic recipe, omitting the rosemary and adding 1 teaspoon
chopped fresh mint instead.

quail's eggs with black olive tapenade

see base recipe page 77

quail's eggs with herb tapenade
Prepare the basic recipe, adding $1/2$ teaspoon chopped fresh marjoram to the tapenade before blending.

crostini with black olive tapenade & quail's eggs
Prepare the basic recipe. Cut 12 thin slices off a small baguette and toast them on both sides until golden. Spread each piece of toast with a thin layer of tapenade and top with a halved quail's egg and chopped parsley.

quail's eggs with creamy tapenade
Prepare the basic recipe, omitting the lemon juice. Gradually stir the tapenade into 115 g/4 oz cream cheese. Then add lemon juice to taste. Add more cream cheese for a lighter flavoured dip.

quail's eggs with lemon & tarragon tapenade
Prepare the basic recipe, adding 2 tablespoons chopped fresh tarragon and the grated rind of 1 lemon with the lemon juice.

smoky spiced almonds

see base recipe page 78

almonds & raisins
Prepare the basic recipe. When the nuts are cool, toss in a handful of fat, juicy raisins.

mixed spiced nuts
Prepare the basic recipe using a mixture of plain unsalted nuts, such as almonds, cashew nuts and pecans.

toasted nuts & raisins
Prepare the basic recipe using a mixture of plain unsalted nuts, such as almonds, cashews and blanched hazelnuts, and omitting the paprika. When the nuts are cool, toss in a handful of fat, juicy raisins.

curried cashews
Prepare the basic recipe using cashew nuts instead of almonds, and garam masala in place of the paprika.

toasted nuts & seeds
Prepare the basic recipe using a mixture of nuts and seeds such as almonds, cashew nuts, pecans, pumpkin seeds and sunflower seeds.

variations

garlic mushrooms

see base recipe page 81

spicy garlic mushrooms
Prepare the basic recipe, adding a good pinch of dried chilli flakes with the mushrooms.

garlic mushrooms and chives
Prepare the basic recipe, omitting the thyme. Serve the mushrooms sprinkled with 1 tablespoon snipped fresh chives.

garlic mushrooms with sherry & oregano
Prepare the basic recipe using sherry in place of the white wine and adding $1/2$ teaspoon chopped fresh oregano in place of the thyme.

creamy garlic mushrooms
Prepare the basic recipe, then stir 1 tablespoon double cream into the mushrooms before serving. Best served hot or warm.

garlic mushrooms with bay
Prepare the basic recipe, adding a bay leaf to the pan with the wine and thyme. Leave the bay with the mushrooms while they are cooling, then remove it before serving.

spicy prawn skewers

see base recipe page 82

chilli prawns
Prepare the basic recipe, adding 1 finely chopped seeded red chilli to the marinade.

sweet chilli prawns
Prepare the basic recipe, using 2 tablespoons sweet chilli sauce in place of the lime rind and juice.

coconut prawns
Prepare the basic recipe. Before cooking, roll the skewered prawns in 2 tablespoons desiccated coconut, then grill as before.

coriander prawns
Prepare the basic recipe, sprinkling the cooked prawns with 1 tablespoon chopped fresh coriander instead of the mint before serving.

prosciutto-wrapped asparagus with lemon mayo

see base recipe page 85

veggie roast asparagus with lemon mayonnaise
Prepare the basic recipe, omitting the prosciutto.

prosciutto-wrapped asparagus with garlic mayonnaise
Prepare the basic recipe, adding 1 small crushed garlic clove to the
mayonnaise and using chopped fresh parsley instead of chives.

prosciutto-wrapped asparagus with caper mayonnaise
Prepare the basic recipe, adding 1 teaspoon chopped capers to the
mayonnaise.

prosciutto-wrapped asparagus with coriander mayonnaise
Prepare the basic recipe, using grated lime rind and juice in place of the
lemon rind and juice, and 1 tablespoon chopped fresh coriander in place of
the chives.

prosciutto-wrapped asparagus with spicy mayonnaise
Prepare the basic recipe, using $1/2$ to 1 teaspoon harissa paste in place of
the chives.

bocconcini with mint & chilli

see base recipe page 86

bocconcini with fennel seeds
Prepare the basic recipe, adding $1/2$ teaspoon lightly crushed fennel seeds.

bocconcini with garlic
Prepare the basic recipe, adding $1/2$ crushed garlic clove.

bocconcini with basil & chilli
Prepare the basic recipe, adding a small handful of torn fresh basil leaves in place of the mint.

bocconcini with sage & chilli
Prepare the basic recipe using $1/2$ teaspoon chopped fresh sage in place of the mint.

variations

tomato & mozzarella skewers

see base recipe page 89

tomato, mozzarella & olive skewers
Prepare the basic recipe, adding a pitted black olive to each cocktail stick.

tomato & mozzarella skewers with rocket
Prepare the basic recipe, threading 1 or 2 rocket leaves on to each
cocktail stick.

tomato, mozzarella & avocado skewers
Peel and stone half an avocado, then slice the flesh into 20 bite-size pieces.
Prepare the basic recipe, adding a cube of avocado to each cocktail stick.

tomato & mozzarella skewers with red onion
Cut half an onion into quarters, then separate into layers. Prepare the basic
recipe, threading a slice of red onion on to each cocktail stick.

variations

feta & watermelon spikes

see base recipe page 90

feta, watermelon & olive spikes
Prepare the basic recipe, adding a pitted black olive to each cocktail stick.

feta & cantaloupe spikes
Prepare the basic recipe, using cataloupe melon in place of the watermelon.

brie & grape spikes
Following the basic method, thread each cocktail stick with a cube of brie
and a large black seedless grape in place of the watermelon and feta.
Omit the lime juice.

blue cheese & pear spikes
Peel, core and slice 2 ripe pears into 24 thin wedges. Following the basic
method, thread cocktail sticks with a cube of blue cheese and a slice of pear.
Omit the lime juice.

blue cheese & fig spikes
Prepare 4 figs, slicing each into 6 wedges. Following the basic method,
thread cocktail sticks with a cube of blue cheese and a wedge of fig.
Omit the lime juice.

big bites

One look at these big tempting treats and your

guests will be begging for the recipes. Serve them

when your guests are starving hungry, to keep them

going until the main meal.

spicy chicken wings

see variations page 117

Golden fried chicken wings are everyone's favourite and great for a party snack to offer before the main food event. For a more formal meal, serve these with dressed salad leaves and ketchup or another dipping sauce.

2 tbsp plain flour
2 tsp cayenne pepper
Salt

12 chicken wings
Sunflower oil, for deep-frying

Put the flour, cayenne pepper and a good pinch of salt in a polythene bag and shake to mix. Add the chicken wings and shake to coat them in the seasoned flour.

Pour oil into a deep pan until it is two-thirds full. Heat to 190°C/375°F or until a cube of bread turns brown in about 1 minute. Add the chicken wings, 3 to 4 at a time, and fry for about 10 minutes until golden brown and cooked through.

Drain the wings on kitchen paper and keep the cooked batches hot while you cook the remaining chicken wings in the same way. Serve hot.

Makes 12

cheese garlic bread

see variations page 118

Richly flavoured garlic bread makes a feel-good starter when you need a little treat. Serve these little breads before an Italian main course or offer them from a platter with drinks at a party.

for the dough

200 g/7 oz cups strong white bread flour
1 tsp easy blend dried yeast
1/2 tsp salt
1 tbsp olive oil
120 ml/4 fl oz warm water

for the topping

2 tbsp olive oil
2 garlic cloves, crushed
150 g/5 oz mozzarella cheese, thinly sliced
Ground black pepper
Chopped fresh parsley, for sprinkling

For the dough: combine the flour, yeast and salt in a bowl, and make a well in the middle. Pour in the oil and water and mix to a soft dough. Turn out on to a lightly floured surface and knead for 5 to 10 minutes until smooth and elastic. Place in a clean oiled bowl, cover with oiled clear film and leave to rise in a warm place for about 1 hour, until doubled in size.

Preheat the oven to 220°C/425°F/Gas Mark 7. Lightly grease a baking sheet. Divide the dough into 8 pieces and roll them into rounds or ovals. Place slightly apart on the baking sheet.

Mix the oil and garlic, then drizzle it over the breads. Top with the cheese, season with pepper and bake for about 12 minutes, until golden. Serve at once, sprinkled with parsley.

Makes 8

mini pizzas with sweet peppers & mozzarella

see variations page 119

These delicious mini pizzas, topped with a rich sweet pepper sauce, are a great twist on the classic tomato pizza.

1 quantity bread dough (see Cheese garlic
    bread, page 103)
2 tbsp olive oil
2 garlic cloves, crushed
2 red peppers, seeded and chopped

1 handful basil leaves
1 tsp balsamic vinegar
5 $^1/_2$ oz mozzarella, sliced
2 handfuls rocket
Salt and ground black pepper

Prepare the bread dough and leave to rise. Meanwhile, heat the oil in a frying pan. Add the garlic and peppers and fry gently for about 20 minutes, stirring frequently until tender. Transfer the peppers to a food processor, add the basil and balsamic vinegar, and process until smooth. Season to taste and set aside.

Preheat the oven to 220°C/425°F/Gas Mark 7. Grease a baking sheet. Knead the risen dough briefly, cut it into eight and roll into rounds. Place, slightly apart, on the baking sheet. Spread about 1 tablespoon of the pepper mixture over each dough round, then top with 1 to 2 slices of mozzarella and season with pepper. Bake for about 10 minutes until golden and bubbling. Top the mini pizzas with rocket leaves and serve immediately.

Makes 8

deep-fried risotto balls with melting mozzarella

see variations page 120

These rich, creamy risotto balls filled with basil and melting mozzarella are an indulgent feast of an appetiser. Serve them with a fresh, tangy tomato or fruit salsa.

2 tbsp olive oil
1 small onion, finely chopped
1 garlic clove, crushed
140 g/5 oz risotto rice
80 ml/3 fl oz white wine
400 ml/14 fl oz boiling vegetable or
    chicken stock

28 g/1 oz grated Parmesan cheese
2 tbsp chopped flat-leaf parsley
85 g/3 oz mozzarella cheese, cut into 12 small
    cubes
12 large basil leaves
Sunflower oil, for deep-frying
Salt and freshly ground black pepper

Heat the oil in a large saucepan. Fry the onion and garlic for 4 minutes, until slightly soft but not browned. Add the rice and stir for 2 minutes. Pour in the wine and simmer, stirring, until absorbed. Add the stock and bubble gently, stirring often, for 20 minutes, until thick, creamy and the rice is tender. Stir in the Parmesan and parsley and season to taste. Set aside to cool.

Divide the rice into twelve portions. Wrap each cube of mozzarella in a basil leaf and enclose in a portion of rice. Leave to stand for at least 30 minutes to firm up. Heat the oil for deep-frying to 190°C/375°F or until a cube of bread turns brown in about 1 minute. Fry the risotto balls for about 3 minutes, until crisp and golden. Drain on kitchen paper and serve hot.

Serves 4

sun-dried tomato frittata

see variations page 121

This thick, Italian-style omelette is delicious served in wedges as a chunky snack with pre-dinner drinks or with a salad for a formal appetiser.

2 tbsp olive oil
1 Spanish onion, thinly sliced
Salt and ground black pepper
1 tsp fresh thyme leaves

6 sun-dried tomatoes in oil, drained and sliced
28 g/1 oz freshly grated Parmesan cheese
6 eggs, beaten

Heat the oil in a large frying pan. Add the onion, sprinkle with a little salt and the thyme, and fry gently for about 15 minutes. Stir in the tomatoes and season to taste.

Stir the Parmesan into the eggs and season with black pepper. Pour the egg mixture over the onions and cook gently for 5 to 10 minutes until the frittata is firm but still moist on top. Lift the edges of the frittata occasionally to allow uncooked egg to run underneath.

Preheat the grill. Brown the top of the frittata under the grill for 3 to 5 minutes. Serve hot, warm or at room temperature, cut into wedges.

Serves 6

caramelised onion & anchovy squares

see variations page 122

Based on the classic French pissaladière, these melting squares of puff pastry make a chunky, satisfying appetiser to hand around with drinks.

2 tbsp olive oil
1 large Spanish onion, halved and thinly sliced
Salt and black pepper
1 tsp fresh thyme leaves, plus extra to serve
2 tsp brown sugar

375 g/13 oz packet ready-rolled puff pastry
55 g/2 oz can anchovy fillets, drained and
halved lengthways

Heat the oil in a frying pan. Add the onion, season and sprinkle with thyme. Cook gently, stirring occasionally, for about 20 minutes, until meltingly soft. Add the sugar and cook for 10 minutes, stirring frequently, until the onion is golden and sticky. Check the seasoning.

Preheat the oven to 190°C/375°F/Gas Mark 5. Unroll the pastry on to a baking sheet. Spread the onion on the pastry, then add the anchovy fillets in a lattice pattern on top.

Bake for about 25 minutes, until the pastry is crisp and golden. Cut the pastry into 12 squares or rectangles and serve hot, warm or at room temperature, sprinkled with more fresh thyme.

Makes 12

potato wedges with crème fraîche & pesto dip

see variations page 123

These are firm favourites with drinks or for a laid-back dinner. Depending on the pesto, you may need to add a teaspoonful more to the dip: taste it first and add a little more pesto if you like.

2 large potatoes (about 600 g/1 lb 5 oz)
2 tbsp olive oil
Salt and ground black pepper

120 ml/4 fl oz crème fraîche
About 1 tbsp green pesto

Preheat the oven to 190°C/375°F/Gas Mark 5. Cut the potatoes into chunky wedges and place in a roasting tin in a single layer. Drizzle with the oil, season with salt and pepper and toss to combine.

Bake the potatoes for 30 to 35 minutes, until golden and tender, shaking and turning them once or twice.

Meanwhile, mix the crème fraîche and pesto in a serving bowl, and season with black pepper. Serve the freshly cooked potato wedges with the dip.

Serves 4

baked camembert

see variations page 124

This recipe is a stunningly simple twist on the classic Swiss fondue. It's perfect in winter, when everyone's cold and hungry.

1 camembert in a wooden box   **1 medium baguette**

Preheat the oven to 190°C/375°F/Gas Mark 5. Discard the waxed paper from around the cheese and return it to its box. Place on a baking sheet and bake for about 20 minutes.

Cut the baguette into bite-size chunks. Transfer the cheese in its box to a serving plate. Break a hole in the crust of the cheese and invite everyone to spike chunks of bread on forks and dunk them into the melted cheese.

Serves 4

grilled polenta with blue cheese & rocket

see variations page 125

This hearty appetizer is particularly good in winter when you need something filling to warm you up. Quick-cook polenta speeds up the preparation but regular polenta can be used instead, prepared following the instructions on the packet.

475 ml/16 fl oz water
1/4 tsp salt
125 g/4 1/2 oz quick-cook polenta
1 tbsp olive oil, plus extra for brushing
2 tsp balsamic vinegar

1/2 tsp wholegrain mustard
55 g/2 oz gorgonzola or other blue cheese, thinly sliced
2 handfuls rocket
Ground black pepper

Bring the water and salt to the boil in a large saucepan. Slowly add the polenta, stirring, and cook for about 3 minutes, until the polenta is thick. Spread out the polenta on a board or tray to 1.5 cm/3/4 in thick, then cool. Whisk the oil with the vinegar and mustard; set aside.

Preheat a griddle pan. Using a 6.5-cm/2 3/4-in cookie cutter, cut the polenta into eight rounds and brush each side with oil. Cook on the griddle for 4 to 5 minutes, until charred with dark lines. Flip over, top with blue cheese and cook for a further 3 to 4 minutes. Transfer to plates, top with rocket and drizzle the dressing over. Grind a little black pepper over the polenta and serve.

Serves 4

variations

spicy chicken wings

see base recipe page 101

hot ginger chicken wings
Prepare the basic recipe, adding 1 teaspoon ground ginger to the flour.

smoky chicken wings
Prepare the basic recipe, adding 2 teaspoons smoked paprika to the flour in place of the cayenne pepper.

warmly spiced chicken wings
Prepare the basic recipe, adding 2 teaspoons ground cumin, 2 teaspoons ground coriander, 1 teaspoon paprika and $1/2$ teaspoon dried chilli flakes to the flour in place of the cayenne pepper.

curried chicken wings
Prepare the basic recipe, adding 2 teaspoons curry powder to the flour.

variations

cheese garlic bread

see base recipe page 103

plain garlic bread
Prepare the basic dough rounds and slash the top of each one several times with a sharp knife. Bake for about 12 minutes. Meanwhile, mix 55 g/2 oz soft butter with 2 crushed garlic cloves and season with black pepper. When the breads are cooked, spread with garlic butter and sprinkle with parsley.

herb & cheese garlic bread
Prepare the basic recipe, sprinkling the breads with fresh thyme leaves or snipped chives, instead of parsley.

cheese garlic bread with pesto
Prepare the basic recipe, spreading about $1/2$ teaspoon pesto on each dough round before drizzling with the garlic oil.

cheese garlic bread with chilli
Prepare the basic recipe, sprinkling a good pinch of dried chilli flakes over each bread before baking.

mini pizzas with sweet peppers & mozzarella

see base recipe page 104

sweet pepper pizza with spicy sausage
Prepare the basic recipe, scattering a few slices of chorizo or other spicy sausage on top before baking. Serve with or without rocket.

sweet pepper pizza with char-grilled courgettes
Slice a courgette and brush with olive oil, then cook on a griddle pan for about 4 minutes on each side, until charred and tender. Prepare the basic pizza recipe, scattering over the courgette slices before baking. Serve without rocket.

sweet pepper pizza with olives
Prepare the basic recipe, scattering a few olives on top of each pizza before baking. Serve with or without rocket.

sweet pepper pizza with capers & pine nuts
Prepare the basic recipe, sprinkling the pizzas with 2 teaspoons rinsed capers and 1 tablespoon pine nuts before baking. Serve with or without rocket.

variations

deep-fried risotto balls with melting mozzarella

see base recipe page 107

risotto balls with chives & mozzarella
Prepare the basic recipe, adding 2 tablespoons snipped fresh chives in place of the parsley. Omit the basil leaves from the filling.

risotto balls with sage & mozzarella
Prepare the basic recipe, adding 2 teaspoons chopped fresh sage in place of the parsley. Omit the basil leaves from the filling.

risotto balls with melting blue cheese
Prepare the basic recipe, using cubes of blue cheese in place of the mozzarella. Omit the basil leaves from the filling.

herbed risotto balls with melting mozzarella
Prepare the basic recipe, stirring 2 tablespoons snipped fresh chives and 2 teaspoons chopped fresh mint into the risotto with the parsley.

variations

sun-dried tomato frittata

see base recipe page 108

leek & sun-dried tomato frittata
Prepare the basic recipe, using 2 sliced leeks in place of the Spanish onion.

roasted pepper frittata
Prepare the basic recipe, adding 3 sliced, bottled roast peppers along with the tomatoes.

sun-dried tomato & sage frittata
Prepare the basic recipe, omitting the thyme and adding $1/2$ teaspoon chopped fresh sage to the beaten eggs.

spicy sun-dried tomato frittata
Prepare the basic recipe, cooking 1 to 2 seeded and chopped fresh red chillies with the onions.

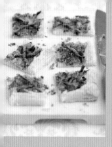

variations

caramelised onion & anchovy squares

see base recipe page 111

caramelised onion & anchovy squares with sultanas
Prepare the basic recipe and sprinkle a handful of sultanas over the tart about 10 minutes before the end of the cooking time.

caramelised onion & anchovy squares with parmesan shavings
Prepare the basic recipe, scattering the squares with Parmesan shavings just before serving.

caramelised onion & anchovy squares with olives
Prepare the basic recipes, scattering a handful of pitted black olives over the tart before baking.

caramelised onion & anchovy squares with oregano
Prepare the basic recipe, using oregano in place of the thyme.

caramelised onion squares with prosciutto
Snip 4 slices of prosciutto into pieces. Prepare the basic recipe, omitting the anchovies and scatter the prosciutto over the top about 10 minutes before the end of the cooking time.

variations

potato wedges with crème fraîche & pesto dip

see base recipe page 112

spicy potato wedges
Prepare the basic recipe, adding 1 teaspoon crushed dried chilli and
1 teaspoon ground cumin to the oil before drizzling it over the potatoes.

potato wedges with tarragon mayonnaise
Prepare the basic recipe, using mayonnaise in place of the crème fraîche and
adding 2 tablespoons chopped fresh tarragon and 1 teaspoon grated lemon
rind instead of the pesto.

potato wedges with red pesto dip
Prepare the basic recipe, using red pesto in place of green pesto.

potato wedges with lemon mayonnaise
Prepare the basic recipe, using mayonnaise in place of the crème fraîche and
adding 1 teaspoon grated lemon rind and 2 teaspoons lemon juice instead
of the pesto.

potato wedges with spicy lemon mayonnaise
Prepare the basic recipe, using mayonnaise in place of the crème fraîche and
adding 2 teaspoons grated lemon rind and several good splashes of Tabasco
instead of the pesto.

variations

baked camembert

see base recipe page 115

baked camembert with new potatoes
Prepare the basic recipe, serving the cheese with boiled baby new potatoes
in place of the baguette.

baked camembert with grissini
Prepare the basic recipe, serving the cheese with chunky grissini instead
of the bread.

baked camembert with cherry tomatoes
Prepare the basic recipe, serving the cheese with cherry tomatoes in place of
the bread.

baked camembert with garlic toasts
Prepare the basic recipe. Instead of serving the baguette in chunks, slice it
and toast on both sides until golden. Rub each slice with a cut clove of
garlic and serve.

baked vacherin
Prepare the basic recipe, using a vacherin in place of the camembert.

grilled polenta with blue cheese & rocket

see base recipe page 116

grilled polenta with blue cheese & baby spinach leaves
Prepare the basic recipe, using baby spinach leaves in place of the rocket.

grilled polenta with blue cheese & cherry tomatoes
Prepare the basic recipe, topping each polenta slice with a few halved cherry tomatoes.

grilled polenta with blue cheese & pear
Prepare the basic recipe, topping each slice with a wedge or two of peeled, cored pear.

grilled polenta with blue cheese & fig
Prepare the basic recipe, topping each slice with a wedge or two of fresh fig.

tapas tasters

Designed as little morsels to serve with drinks, these
Spanish-style appetisers are perfect for whetting
the appetite and are guaranteed to get a party
going with a swing. Prepare a selection and let
guests pick and choose.

mini meatballs

see variations page 142

These richly flavoured meatballs make a tempting informal appetiser. Serve with cocktail sticks for skewering them, if offering them with drinks, or with chunks of bread at the table for mopping up the luscious sauce.

175 g/6 oz lean minced beef
$1/4$ onion, grated
$1/2$ garlic clove, crushed
1 tsp chopped fresh oregano

1 tbsp grated Parmesan cheese
1 tbsp olive oil
225 g/8 oz tomatoes, peeled and chopped
Salt and ground black pepper

Combine the beef, onion, garlic, half the oregano and the Parmesan in a bowl. Season well and mix thoroughly. Roll the mixture into about 20 bite-size balls.

Heat the oil in a large, non-stick frying pan. Add the meatballs and cook, stirring them gently to brown them all over. Work in batches if necessary, removing browned meatballs as they are ready. When all are browned, return all the meatballs to the pan.

Add the tomatoes and remaining thyme, season and simmer gently for about 20 minutes, until the meatballs are cooked and tender. Serve hot or warm.

Serves 4

grilled mussels

see variations page 143

This simple yet sophisticated appetiser has a distinctly Spanish feel and is perfect for whetting the appetite.

500 g/1 lb 2 oz mussels, cleaned
4 tbsp dried breadcrumbs
3 tbsp freshly grated Parmesan cheese
2 garlic cloves, crushed

2 tbsp chopped fresh parsley
$2^1/_2$ tbsp olive oil
Ground black pepper

Check the mussels, discarding any that are open and do not close when sharply tapped. Put the closed mussels in a large pan, add 3 tablespoons water, cover tightly and cook over a high heat for about 5 minutes, shaking the pan frequently, until the mussels have opened.

Discard any unopened shells. Snap off and discard the top shell of each mussel and arrange the shells with mussels in a flameproof dish.

Preheat the grill. Combine the breadcrumbs, cheese, garlic, parsley and oil, and season with black pepper. Spoon the crumb mixture on to the mussels, then grill them for about 2 minutes until golden and bubbling. Serve immediately.

Serves 4

garlic & chilli prawns

see variations page 144

Serve these delectable prawns with chunks of crusty bread for soaking up the garlic and chilli-infused oil.

3 tbsp olive oil
1 garlic clove, crushed
$1/4$ tsp dried chilli flakes

20 raw tiger prawns (with shells on)
Chunks of crusty bread, to serve

Heat the oil in a frying pan and fry the garlic and chilli for about 1 minute, until aromatic. Add the prawns and cook for a further 3 to 4 minutes, turning them occasionally, until they are pink and cooked through.

Transfer the prawns to plates and serve immediately with the oil from the pan drizzled over and chunks of bread to mop it up.

Serves 4

green pea tortilla

see variations page 145

Tortilla is great to serve in bite-size pieces with drinks or with a simple salad as a more formal appetiser.

2 tbsp olive oil
2 Spanish onions, halved and finely sliced
Salt and ground black pepper

300 g/10^1/$_2$ oz frozen peas, thawed
6 eggs
2 tsp chopped fresh mint

Heat the oil in a 22.5-cm/9-in non-stick frying pan. Add the onion, sprinkle with a little salt and fry gently for about 25 minutes, until tender and collapsed. Season to taste, then stir in the peas.

Beat the eggs with the mint and seasoning, then pour them over the onions and peas. Cook gently for about 10 minutes, pulling away the edges of the tortilla as it sets to allow the uncooked egg to run underneath.

Meanwhile, preheat the grill. When the tortilla is firm but still moist on top, brown the top under the grill for about 5 minutes, until golden and set. Leave to cool for a few minutes.

Cover the pan with a plate and carefully invert both pan and plate. Remove the pan. Place another plate on top of the tortilla and invert both plates and tortilla to turn it right-side up. Serve warm or at room temperature, cut into wedges or bite-size pieces.

Serves 8

pinchos

see variations page 146

These salty and piquant little skewers are served with drinks all over Spain. They're the perfect light-bite to serve before a big meal.

12 canned or marinated anchovy fillets, drained   **12 cornichons**
12 caper berries

Roll the anchovy fillets into coils and thread each one on to a separate cocktail stick.

Add a caper berry and cornichon to each stick and serve.

Makes 12

salt cod fritters with garlic mayonnaise

see variations page 147

Salt cod needs to be soaked before cooking, so remember to leave enough time for preparing this recipe. Drain and change the water a couple of times during soaking.

200 ml/7 fl oz milk
225 g/8 oz salt cod, soaked in cold water for 24
   hours, rinsed and drained
225 g/8 oz potatoes, cooked and mashed
1 shallot, finely chopped
2 tbsp chopped fresh parsley
Ground black pepper
Juice of $1/2$ lemon
2 tbsp plain flour

1 egg, beaten
40 g/$1^1/_4$ oz dried breadcrumbs
Sunflower oil, for frying

for the garlic mayonnaise

120 ml/4 fl oz mayonnaise
$1^1/_2$ garlic cloves, crushed
1 tsp lemon juice

Bring the milk to a simmer. Add the cod and poach it gently for about 10 minutes, until it flakes easily. Flake the flesh into a bowl, discarding skin and bones. Mix in the potatoes, shallot, parsley, black pepper and lemon juice to taste. Shape the mixture into 8 to 12 patties, dust with flour, dip in egg, then coat in breadcrumbs. Chill for at least 30 minutes. Mix the mayonnaise, garlic and lemon juice in a bowl, add pepper and set aside. Heat about 2.5 cm/1 in sunflower oil in a frying pan. Fry the patties (in batches if necessary) for about 3 minutes each side, until golden. Drain on kitchen paper. Serve with the garlic mayonnaise.

Serves 4

garlic spinach with pine nuts

see variations page 148

This classic tapas recipe is delicious served with a selection of other dishes to start a meal. Choose simple complementary dishes, such as marinated olives and artichoke hearts, and serve with chunks of crusty bread.

2 tbsp olive oil
3 tbsp pine nuts
2 garlic cloves, crushed

250 g/9 oz spinach
Salt and ground black pepper

Heat the oil in a large non-stick saucepan and fry the pine nuts for 2 to 3 minutes, until golden. Add the garlic and fry gently for about 30 seconds.

Add the spinach and cook, tossing and turning the leaves, for about 3 minutes, until wilted. Season with salt and pepper and serve immediately.

Serves 4

spicy fried potatoes & chorizo

see variations page 149

A simple twist on the classic spicy Spanish potatoes, patatas bravas, these piping hot potatoes are fabulous to serve with a big jug of sangria. Choose really tiny potatoes if you can, or cut larger ones in half, and provide cocktail sticks for picking them up.

400 g/14 oz new potatoes
3 tbsp olive oil
200 g/7 oz chorizo, cut into bite-size chunks
2 garlic cloves, crushed

$1/2$ teaspoon dried chilli flakes
Chopped fresh parsely, for sprinkling
Salt

Cut any larger potatoes in half to make bite-size pieces. Cook the potatoes in boiling salted water for about 10 minutes, until tender. Drain well, return them to the pan and leave them off the heat to steam dry in the heat of the pan.

Heat the oil in a large frying pan. Add the potatoes and fry for about 5 minutes, turning them occasionally. Add the chorizo and continue frying the mixture until the potatoes are crisp and golden.

Sprinkle with the garlic and chilli, and cook for a further 1 to 2 minutes. Transfer the potatoes to a serving dish. Sprinkle with a little salt and parsley and serve.

Serves 4

mini meatballs

see base recipe page 127

mini meatballs with roast peppers
Prepare the basic recipe, adding 1 sliced bottled roast pepper with
the tomatoes.

mini meatballs with chilli
Prepare the basic recipe, adding $1/4$ teaspoon dried chilli flakes to the sauce.

mini meatballs with thyme
Prepare the basic recipe, using fresh thyme in place of the oregano.

mini meatballs with basil
Prepare the basic recipe, using a small handful of fresh basil in place of
the thyme.

mini meatballs with sun-dried tomatoes
Prepare the basic recipe, adding 3 sliced, drained sun-dried tomatoes in oil
to the sauce.

grilled mussels

see base recipe page 129

grilled mussels with chives
Prepare the basic recipe, using snipped chives in place of the parsley.

grilled mussels with shallot
Prepare the basic recipe, adding 1 finely chopped shallot to the
topping mixture.

grilled mussels with tarragon
Prepare the basic recipe, using 1 tablespoon chopped fresh tarragon in place
of the parsley.

spicy grilled mussels
Prepare the basic recipe, adding a good pinch of cayenne pepper to the
topping mixture in place of black pepper.

variations

garlic & chilli prawns

see base recipe page 130

garlic prawns
Prepare the basic recipe, omitting the chilli and seasoning with ground black pepper instead.

zesty garlic & chilli prawns
Prepare the basic recipe, sprinkling $1/4$ teaspoon grated lemon rind over the prawns before serving.

garlic & chilli prawns with parsley
Prepare the basic recipe, sprinkling 1 to 2 tablespoon chopped parsley over the prawns before serving.

garlic & chilli prawns with chives
Prepare the basic recipe, sprinkling 1 tablespoon snipped chives over the prawns before serving.

variations

green pea tortilla

see base recipe page 133

traditional tortilla
Prepare the basic recipe using 300 g/10^1/$_2$ oz sliced cooked potatoes in place of the peas, and 1 teaspoon fresh thyme leaves in place of the mint.

green pea tortilla with spicy sausage
Prepare the basic recipe, adding 55 g/2 oz thinly sliced chorizo with the onions.

green pea tortilla with sun-dried tomato
Prepare the basic recipe, adding 4 drained, sliced sun-dried tomatoes in oil with the peas.

broad bean tortilla
Prepare the basic recipe, using lightly cooked broad beans in place of the peas.

variations

pinchos

see base recipe page 134

simple pinchos
Prepare the basic recipe, omitting the cornichons.

spicy pinchos
Prepare the basic recipe, using pickled chillies in place of the cornichons.

veggie pinchos
Prepare the basic recipe, using strips of bottled roast pepper in place of the anchovies.

spicy veggie pinchos
Prepare the basic recipe, using strips of bottled roast pepper in place of the anchovies and pickled chillies in place of the cornichons.

variations

salt cod fritters with garlic mayonnaise

see base recipe page 137

salt cod fritters with lemon mayonnaise
Prepare the basic recipe, adding $1/4$ teaspoon grated lemon rind to the mayonnaise in place of the garlic.

salt cod fritters with herb mayonnaise
Prepare the basic recipe, adding 1 tablespoon snipped fresh chives and 2 teaspoons chopped fresh tarragon to the mayonnaise instead of the garlic.

salt cod fritters with pesto mayonnaise
Prepare the basic recipe, adding 1 tablespoon pesto to the mayonnaise in place of the garlic and lemon juice.

salt cod fritters with tomato salsa
Prepare the basic recipe, serving the fritters with tomato salsa instead of the mayonnaise.

variations

garlic spinach with pine nuts

see base recipe page 138

garlic spinach with pine nuts & raisins
Prepare the basic recipe, and toss in 2 tablespoons raisins before serving.

garlic spinach with pine nuts & chorizo
Prepare the basic recipe, frying 55 g/2 oz chopped chorizo with the pine nuts.

garlic spinach with pine nuts & chilli
Prepare the basic recipe, adding a generous pinch of dried chilli flakes with the spinach.

lemon & garlic spinach with pine nuts
Prepare the basic recipe, adding a good squeeze of lemon juice, to taste, with the seasoning.

garlic spinach with pine nuts & dill
Prepare the basic recipe, adding 2 tablespoons chopped fresh dill just before serving.

variations

spicy fried potatoes & chorizo

see base recipe page 141

spicy potatoes
Prepare the basic recipe, omitting the chorizo.

fried potatoes with chorizo & marjoram
Prepare the basic recipe, sprinkling the potatoes with 1 teaspoon chopped
fresh marjoram in place of the parsley.

fried potatoes with mayonnaise
Prepare the basic recipe and serve with a dish of garlic mayonnaise
for dunking.

fried potatoes with lemon mayonnaise
Prepare the basic recipe and serve with lemon mayonnaise. To make lemon
mayonnaise, stir 1 teaspoon grated lemon rind, 2 teaspoons lemon juice and
a good splash of Tabasco into 120 ml/4 fl oz mayonnaise.

amazing meze

Traditionally served with drinks, these fabulously
flavoured snacks make wonderful appetizers. From
dips and salads to little edible parcels and skewered
meatballs, you'll find something for every guest
and for every occasion.

feta filo pastries

see variations page 167

These crisp, golden pastries are surprisingly easy to make. Serve them with a selection of meze, nestled on dressed salad leaves, or as a bite-size snack with drinks.

200 g/7 oz feta cheese, crumbled
1¹/₂ tbsp chopped fresh mint
2 eggs, beaten

Ground black pepper
8 sheets filo pastry
50 g/2 oz butter, melted

Preheat the oven to 190°C/375°F/Gas Mark 5. Lightly grease a baking sheet.

Put the feta, mint and eggs in a bowl, season with pepper and mix well, mashing the cheese with the eggs.

Lay the filo sheets on a board and cut in half to make sixteen strips. Take one strip and cover the rest with a damp cloth. Brush the strip with butter and place about 1 tablespoon of the feta mixture at one end, spreading it slightly to make a sausage shape. Roll the cheese and pastry over once or twice, then fold over the side edges and roll up all the way to make a sealed cigar-shaped pastry. Place on the baking sheet and brush with more butter. Make the remaining pastries in the same way.

Bake the pastries for about 15 minutes, until crisp and golden. Serve hot or transfer to a wire rack and cool, then serve warm or at room temperature.

Makes 16

stuffed vine leaves

see variations page 168

Tender, juicy stuffed vine leaves flavoured with fresh mint, spring onions and lemon juice make a great appetiser. Serve them solo, with drinks, or with other meze, such as marinated olives.

100 g/3^1/$_2$ oz rice, cooked
1 bunch spring onions, finely sliced
2 tbsp chopped fresh mint
3 tbsp olive oil

Juice of 1 lemon
Salt and ground black pepper
20 preserved vine leaves, rinsed
Lemon wedges, to serve

Put the rice, spring onions and mint in a bowl. Pour over 1 tablespoon of the oil, squeeze over half the lemon juice and season to taste with salt and pepper. Mix well.

Lay a leaf on a board. Place a tablespoon of the rice mixture in a mound near the stalk end. Fold the end over and fold over the sides. Then roll up the rice in the leaf to form a tight, neat package. Repeat with the remaining leaves and stuffing. Arrange the rolls in a steamer.

Place the steamer over a pan of simmering water, drizzle the rolls with the remaining oil, cover and steam for about 40 minutes. (Check the water occasionally, adding more if necessary.)

Transfer the vine leaves to a plate, squeeze over a little more lemon juice, then leave to cool. Serve at room temperature, with lemon wedges for squeezing.

Makes 20

baby gem leaves filled with tabbouleh

see variations page 169

Tabbouleh is a zesty, herb-flavoured salad of nutty bulgur, a part-cooked, cracked wheat product that is ready to eat after soaking (and not to be confused with ordinary cracked wheat, which is raw and has to be boiled). Serve these tabbouleh-filled leaves as a formal appetiser at the table, or as casual finger food with drinks.

115 g/4 oz bulgur wheat
Salt and ground black pepper
28 g/1 oz chopped fresh parsley
15 g/^{1}/$_2$ oz chopped fresh mint

2 ripe tomatoes, seeded and diced
2 tbsp olive oil
Juice of ^{1}/$_2$ lemon
12 baby gem lettuce leaves

Put the bulghur wheat in a bowl, add a good pinch of salt and pour boiling water over to cover. Leave to soak for 20 minutes, then drain well.

Combine the bulghur, parsley, mint and tomato in a large bowl, and season with salt and pepper. Drizzle in the oil, squeeze over the lemon juice and toss to combine.

Arrange the lettuce leaves on a serving plate and spoon the salad into them.

Serves 4

garlicky aubergine & tomato stacks

see variations page 170

These pretty Mediterranean vegetable stacks make a lovely appetiser served at the table. Top each one with a fresh basil leaf, if liked.

1 aubergine
2 tbsp olive oil, plus extra for brushing
2 garlic cloves, crushed

450 g/1 lb cherry tomatoes, halved
Handful of fresh basil leaves, torn
Salt and ground black pepper

Heat a griddle pan. Slice the aubergine into twelve 1 cm/1/2 in thick rounds, brush with oil on both sides and season with salt and pepper.

Working in batches, cook the aubergine slices for about 5 minutes on each side, until tender. Transfer to a large dish and keep warm while you cook the remaining slices.

Meanwhile, heat the oil in a pan and fry the garlic for about 1 minute. Add the tomatoes and seasoning, and cook gently for about 10 minutes, until soft. Check the seasoning, toss in the basil and stir to combine.

Arrange the aubergine slices on a platter, top each one with a spoonful of tomatoes and serve immediately.

Serves 4

falafel with yogurt dip

see variations page 171

Be sure to use dried chickpeas for this recipe and not canned ones, otherwise the falafel will fall apart during cooking.

200 g/7 oz dried chickpeas, soaked in cold
    water overnight
1 onion, finely chopped
1 garlic clove, chopped
1 tsp ground cumin
1 tsp ground coriander

Good pinch of cayenne pepper
2 tbsp chopped fresh parsley
120 ml/4 fl oz plain yogurt
1 1/2 tbsp chopped fresh mint
Sunflower oil, for deep-frying
Salt and ground black pepper

Drain the chickpeas and put in a food processor with the onion, garlic, cumin, coriander and cayenne pepper. Process to a smooth paste. Season well, add the parsley and process briefly.

Rinse your hands under cold water. Take a heaped tablespoon of the mixture and shape it into a patty. Repeat with the remaining mixture, pressing it firmly into shape and wetting your hands to prevent the patties from sticking. Leave to stand for 30 minutes.

Meanwhile, combine the yogurt and mint in a serving bowl, season to taste and chill.

Heat about 2.5 cm/1 in oil in a pan. Working in batches, add the falafel and cook for about 5 minutes, turning once or twice, until crisp and golden all over. Drain on kitchen paper and keep warm until all are cooked. Serve hot or warm, with the yogurt dip.

Makes about 16 to serve 4

hummus

see variations page 172

This classic dip from the Middle East is delicious served with wedges of pitta or vegetable sticks, alone or as part of a meze selection.

400 g/14 oz can chickpeas, rinsed and drained
1 garlic clove, crushed
1 tsp ground cumin
1 tsp ground coriander

1 tbsp tahini
3 tbsp olive oil
Juice of $^1/_2$ to $^3/_4$ lemon
Salt and ground black pepper

Put the chickpeas, garlic, cumin, coriander, tahini and oil in a food processor and squeeze in the juice of $^1/_2$ lemon.

Process the mixture to a smooth purée, scraping down the sides of the bowl occasionally. Season and squeeze in more lemon juice to taste.

Spoon the hummus into a bowl and serve.

Serves 4

lamb koftas

see variations page 173

These lightly spiced lamb skewers make a tasty start to any meal. Serve with a tomato salsa and, if you like, offer a chopped vegetable salad as well.

225 g/8 oz lean minced lamb
2 fat spring onions, finely chopped
1 garlic clove, crushed
1 tsp ground cumin
1 tsp ground coriander

$1/4$ tsp cayenne pepper
2 tsp chopped fresh mint
Salt and ground black pepper
Tomato salsa (see page 51), to serve

Soak 8 wooden cocktail sticks in cold water for 15 minutes.

In a bowl, mix the lamb, spring onions, garlic, cumin, coriander, cayenne pepper and mint until thoroughly combined. Season well with the salt and black pepper. Use your hands to mix the ingredients together thoroughly.

Divide the meat into 8 pieces and shape them into small egg-shaped balls. Thread each ball on a cocktail stick and press it out to form a sausage shape. Chill for about 30 minutes.

Preheat the grill. Grill the skewers for 5 to 8 minutes, turning once or twice, until cooked through. Serve with tomato salsa.

Serves 4

grilled halloumi with garlic, lemon & chilli

see variations page 174

This wonderful salty cheese is traditionally served grilled or fried, when it softens to a deliciously chewy texture. You'll find it in supermarkets and Mediterranean food stores.

200 g/7 oz halloumi
1 garlic clove, crushed
1/4 tsp dried chilli flakes

Juice of 1 lemon
2 tbsp olive oil

Slice the cheese into 7 mm/1/4 in thick slices and arrange in a large dish.

Whisk together the garlic, chilli, lemon juice and oil, and pour this over the cheese, turning the slices to coat them. Leave to marinate for at least 1 hour.

Heat a dry, non-stick frying pan or griddle pan. Cook the cheese for 1 to 2 minutes on each side, until golden and sizzling. Serve immediately as the cheese will toughen on cooling.

Serves 4

spiced carrot salad

see variations page 175

This simple carrot salad looks stunning, with its fiery colour, and it makes a deliciously light start to any meal.

450 g/1 lb carrots, finely sliced
Salt
1 small garlic clove, crushed
$1/4$ tsp ground ginger
$1/2$ tsp ground cumin
$1/4$ tsp ground coriander

$1/4$ tsp paprika
Good pinch of cayenne pepper
2 tsp red wine vinegar
$1^1/2$ tbsp olive oil
1 tsp chopped fresh mint, plus extra for
    sprinkling

Put the carrots in a pan with 2 tablespoons water, season with salt, cover tightly, then cook over a low heat, shaking the pan now and again, for about 10 minutes, until tender.

Remove the lid and, if there is any liquid remaining in the pan, cook the carrots, uncovered, for a minute or two until all the liquid has evaporated. Remove from the heat.

Whisk together the garlic, ginger, cumin, coriander, paprika, cayenne pepper, vinegar and oil, and season with salt. Stir in the mint, then pour this dressing over the carrots in the pan. Leave to stand for at least 30 minutes.

To serve, warm the carrots for a few seconds over low heat, if necessary, or serve them at room temperature, sprinkled with a little extra mint.

Serves 4

variations

feta filo pastries

see base recipe page 151

feta pastries with pine nuts
Prepare the basic recipe, adding 1 tablespoon toasted pine nuts to the feta mixture.

feta & spinach pastries
Prepare the basic mixture, stirring in 3 tablespoons thawed and drained chopped spinach when the feta has combined with the eggs.

feta & herb pastries
Prepare the basic recipe, adding 2 teaspoons snipped fresh chives and 2 tablespoons chopped fresh parsley to the feta mixture.

feta & spring onion pastries
Prepare the basic recipe, adding 1 bunch finely sliced spring onions to the feta mixture.

variations

stuffed vine leaves

see base recipe page 153

stuffed vine leaves with dill
Prepare the basic recipe, adding 2 teaspoons chopped fresh dill to the
cooked rice mixture.

spicy vine leaves
Prepare the basic recipe, adding a good pinch of cayenne pepper to the
cooked rice mixture.

stuffed vine leaves with pine nuts
Prepare the basic recipe, adding 1 tablespoon toasted pine nuts to the
cooked rice mixture.

stuffed vine leaves with red onion
Prepare the basic recipe, adding 1 small finely chopped red onion to the
cooked rice mixture.

baby gem leaves filled with tabbouleh

see base recipe page 154

tabbouleh with cucumber
Prepare the basic recipe, adding $1/4$ diced, seeded cucumber with
the tomato.

tabbouleh with spring onions
Prepare the basic recipe, adding 4 thinly sliced spring onions with
the tomato.

tabbouleh with coriander
Prepare the basic recipe, adding 28 g/1 oz chopped fresh coriander in place
of the mint.

tabbouleh with green chilli
Prepare the basic recipe, adding 1 finely chopped, seeded fresh green chilli
with the tomato.

spiced tabbouleh
Prepare the basic recipe, adding $1/4$ teaspoon ground cumin and
$1/4$ teaspoon ground coriander with the tomato.

variations

garlicky aubergine & tomato stacks

see base recipe page 157

spicy aubergine & tomato stacks
Prepare the basic recipe, adding $1/2$ teaspoon dried chilli flakes to
the tomatoes.

aubergine, tomato & olive stacks
Prepare the basic recipe, adding 10 halved black olives to the tomatoes.

aubergine & tomato stacks with feta
Prepare the basic recipe, topping the tomato stacks with crumbled feta.

aubergine & tomato stacks with Parmesan
Prepare the basic recipe, topping the tomato stacks with shavings of
Parmesan cheese.

aubergine & tomato stacks with oregano
Prepare the basic recipe, adding 1 teaspoon fresh oregano leaves with the
tomatoes. Omit the basil.

variations

falafel with yogurt dip

see base recipe page 158

spicy falafel
Prepare the basic recipe, adding $1/4$ teaspoon dried chilli flakes in place of the cayenne pepper.

falafel in pitta pockets
Prepare the basic recipe and serve the falafel in split, warmed pitta breads, with chopped tomato and cucumber, and drizzled with yogurt dressing.

falafel with tomato salsa
Prepare the basic recipe and serve with tomato salsa instead of the yogurt dip.

falafel with cucumber & yogurt dip
Prepare the basic recipe, adding $1/4$ grated, seeded cucumber to the yogurt dip.

falafel with fresh salad
Prepare the basic recipe and serve the falafel and dip with a crunchy lettuce, cucumber and tomato salad.

variations

hummus

see base recipe page 161

avocado hummus
Prepare the basic recipe, adding 1 small, peeled and stoned avocado to the
food processor.

roast pepper hummus
Preheat the oven to 230°C/450°F/Gas Mark 8. Place 1 red pepper on a baking
sheet and bake for about 30 minutes until blackened. Put the pepper in a
bowl, cover with clear film and leave to stand for about 10 minutes. Peel
and seed, then cut the flesh into chunks. Prepare the basic recipe, adding the
red pepper chunks before processing.

hummus with sesame seeds
Prepare the basic recipe, adding 1 tablespoon sesame seeds in place of
the tahini.

hummus with dill
Prepare the basic recipe, sprinkling the hummus with chopped fresh dill
before serving.

spicy hummus
Prepare the basic recipe, adding $1/2$ teaspoon dried chilli flakes.

variations

lamb koftas

see base recipe page 162

lamb kofta wraps
Serve the koftas and tomato salsa wrapped in quartered flour tortillas.

beef koftas
Prepare the basic recipe, using minced beef instead of lamb.

chicken or turkey koftas
Prepare the basic recipe, using minced chicken or turkey instead of lamb.

harissa-spiced lamb koftas
Prepare the basic recipe, using 1 to 2 teaspoon harissa in place of the cumin, coriander and cayenne.

lemon lamb koftas
Prepare the basic recipe, adding the grated rind of $1/2$ lemon with the spices.

variations

grilled halloumi with garlic, lemon & chilli

see base recipe page 165

grilled halloumi with lemon & chilli
Prepare the basic recipe, omitting the garlic.

grilled halloumi with lemon, garlic & oregano
Prepare the basic recipe, adding 1 teaspoon fresh oregano leaves in place of the chilli.

grilled halloumi with lemon & garlic
Prepare the basic recipe, omitting the chilli.

grilled halloumi with cumin, lemon & garlic
Prepare the basic recipe, adding $1/2$ teaspoon crushed cumin seeds in place of the chilli.

grilled halloumi with fennel, chilli & lemon
Prepare the basic recipe, adding $1/2$ teaspoon crushed fennel seeds in place of the garlic.

spiced carrot salad

see base recipe page 166

carrot salad with harissa
Prepare the basic recipe, using 1 teaspoon harissa in place of the paprika and cayenne pepper.

spiced beetroot salad
Prepare the basic recipe, using cooked beetroot in place of the carrots. Thinly slice the cooked beetroot, then simply pour the dressing over and serve at room temperature.

spiced broad bean salad
Prepare the basic recipe, using broad beans instead of carrots. Cook the beans in a pan of boiling water for about 3 minutes, until tender, then drain and dress.

carrot salad with fresh coriander
Prepare the basic recipe, using 1 tablespoon chopped fresh coriander in place of the mint, and sprinkling with more coriander to serve.

asian flavour

A classic Asian meal doesn't start with appetisers, but the fabulous array of snacks that are served at other times of day are perfect before a meal. Serve as cocktail snacks or sit down and enjoy them at the table. For a unique dinner party twist, involve your guests in preparing sushi rolls or duck wraps.

thai crab cakes with chilli vinegar

see variations page 193

These spicy little fish cakes are perfect to start a South-east Asian meal, but they also make a great snack to serve with cocktails.

Two 170-g/6-oz cans crabmeat, drained
2 tsp red curry paste
1 tsp grated fresh root ginger
2 tbsp chopped fresh coriander leaves
$1/2$ tsp Thai fish sauce
1 egg
2 tbsp plain flour
Sunflower oil, for frying

for the chilli vinegar

1 tbsp sugar
50 ml/2 fl oz rice wine vinegar
2 tsp Thai fish sauce
2 fresh red chillies, seeded and sliced

Prepare the chilli vinegar. Put the sugar, vinegar and fish sauce in a pan and warm gently, stirring, until the sugar has dissolved. Pour into a bowl, add the chillies and set aside to cool.

Put the crabmeat, curry paste, ginger, coriander and fish sauce in a bowl, and mix together well using a fork. Stir in the egg, then sprinkle the flour over and mix well to combine. Shape the mixture into 16 small fish cakes.

Heat about 1 tablespoon oil in a non-stick pan. Fry the fish cakes in batches if necessary for 2–3 minutes on each side, until golden. Drain well on kitchen paper and serve hot, with chilli vinegar for dipping.

Makes 16

chicken satay with spicy peanut sauce

see variations page 194

These Indonesian-style skewers are a great way to start a barbecue, and they're equally good cooked and eaten inside – either at the table, or as a pre-dinner nibble.

3 skinless boneless chicken breasts
1 garlic clove, crushed
1 tsp grated fresh root ginger
Grated rind and juice of 1 lime
1 tsp Thai fish sauce

for the peanut sauce

2 tbsp coconut milk
4 tbsp crunchy peanut butter
Juice of $1/2$ lime
$1/4$ tsp dried chilli flakes

Slice each chicken breast into 4 long strips. Combine the garlic, ginger, lime rind and juice and fish sauce and pour over the chicken. Cover and marinate for about 1 hour. Meanwhile, soak 12 bamboo skewers in cold water.

Preheat the grill. Thread a strip of chicken on to each skewer. Cook the chicken for about 3 minutes on each side, until cooked through.

Meanwhile, stir the coconut milk into the peanut butter until smooth and creamy. Stir in the lime juice and chilli. Serve immediately with the chicken satay.

Makes 12

salt & pepper squid

see variations page 195

Crisp and tender, deep-fried squid makes a fabulous start to any meal. If you're serving it with drinks, offer cocktail sticks or pretty spikes to pick up the squid rings.

450 g/1 lb squid, cleaned
Juice of 2 limes
$1/2$ tsp coarse sea salt
1 tbsp ground black pepper

70 g/$2^1/2$ oz rice flour
Sunflower oil, for deep-frying
Lime wedges and sweet chilli sauce, to serve

Pull the head and tentacles from the squid bodies. Discard the plastic-like quills running down inside the body sacs, and slice the bodies into rings. Squeeze the lime juice over, toss to combine, then marinate in the refrigerator for about 15 minutes.

Meanwhile, combine the salt, pepper and rice flour. Drain the squid and pat dry on kitchen paper, then toss the rings in the salt and pepper mixture.

Pour oil into a pan to fill it by two-thirds and heat to 180°C/350°F, or until a cube of bread browns in about 1 minute.

Working in batches, deep-fry the squid for about 1 minute, until crisp and golden. Drain well on kitchen paper and serve freshly cooked, with lime wedges for squeezing over and sweet chilli sauce for dipping.

Serves 4

fruity lamb samosas

see variations page 196

Samosas are traditionally deep-fried but, for a healthier option, these are made with filo pastry and baked.

2 tbsp sunflower oil
1 small onion
2 garlic cloves, crushed
1 1/2 tsp ground cumin
1 1/2 tsp ground coriander
1/4 tsp cayenne pepper

225 g/8 oz minced lamb
2 tsp mango chutney, plus extra to serve
12 sheets filo pastry
50 g/1 3/4 oz butter, melted
Salt and ground black pepper

Preheat the oven to 200°C/400°F/Gas Mark 6. Lightly grease a baking sheet. Heat the oil in a non-stick pan and gently fry the onion and garlic for about 4 minutes. Stir in the spices. Add the lamb and fry, stirring, for 2 to 3 minutes until browned all over. Drain off excess fat, then stir in the mango chutney and season to taste.

Lay a sheet of pastry on a board, brush with butter and fold over lengthways to make a long, double-thick strip. Brush with more butter. Place a heaped spoonful of lamb in the bottom corner of the pastry. Fold pastry and filling over into a triangle. Continue folding the triangle from corner to corner to make a sealed, triangular pastry. Repeat, making 11 more samosas.

Place the samosas on the baking sheet and bake for 15 to 20 minutes, until crisp and golden. Serve with mango chutney for dunking.

Makes 12

sushi rolls

see variations page 197

Traditional sushi is made with a special Japanese short-grained rice, but it can work just as well with sticky jasmine rice, which is more readily available in supermarkets.

200 g/7 oz jasmine or sushi rice
2 tbsp rice vinegar
1 1/2 tsp sugar
1/2 tsp salt
3 nori sheets
Soy sauce and pickled ginger, to serve

for the filling

1 tbsp mayonnaise
1/4 tsp wasabi paste
85 g/3 oz canned crabmeat
1/4 cucumber, seeded and cut into matchstick strips

Put the rice in a pan and add 570 ml/1 pint boiling water. Bring to the boil, reduce the heat, cover and simmer for 12 minutes, until the water is absorbed. Leave to stand off the heat, covered, for 10 minutes. Meanwhile, mix the vinegar, sugar and salt. Turn the rice into a bowl and pour the vinegar over. Fold the dressing into the rice. Leave to cool to room temperature.

Mix the mayonnaise and wasabi, then fold in the crabmeat. Cut the nori in half lengthways to make six sheets. Lay a sheet of nori on a bamboo rolling mat and place a line of rice along one long edge. Spread a little crab mixture and a line of cucumber sticks on the rice. Using the rolling mat, roll up the nori tightly to enclose the filling. Use a sharp knife to slice the roll into 6 smaller sushi rolls. Rinse and wipe the knife between cuts if it becomes sticky. Repeat with the remaining ingredients. Serve with soy sauce for dipping and pickled ginger.

Makes 36

vietnamese crystal rolls

see variations page 198

These rolls are fabulous for whetting the appetite and they are low-fat too. For a fun do-it-yourself appetizer, place all the ingredients in bowls so that guests can assemble the rolls themselves.

12 Vietnamese rice paper wrappers
2 handfuls beansprouts
1 carrot, cut into matchstick strips
$1/2$ cucumber, seeded and cut into matchstick strips
115 g/4 oz firm tofu, cut into small cubes

3 spring onions, thinly sliced
2 garlic cloves, finely chopped
40 g/$1^1/2$ oz peanuts, chopped
Soy sauce and sweet chilli sauce, for drizzling
Handful of fresh coriander leaves

Fill a large, shallow bowl with water. Dip a rice paper wrapper in the water for about 20 seconds, until softened. Lay it on a plate.

Sprinkle beansprouts down the middle of the wrapper. Sprinkle carrot, cucumber, tofu, spring onions, garlic and peanuts on top. Drizzle a little soy sauce and sweet chilli sauce over, and then top with a few coriander leaves.

Fold the short ends of the wrapper over to enclose the filling, then roll up tightly to make a sealed parcel. Repeat with the remaining wrappers and filling, and serve immediately.

Makes 12

peking duck wraps

see variations page 199

These mini duck wraps make a really pretty appetizer, either as finger food with drinks or arranged on a plate with a few salad leaves.

2 boneless duck breasts
Salt
12 Chinese pancakes, halved
2 tbsp hoisin sauce
6 spring onions, shredded
1/4 cucumber, seeded and cut into matchstick
   strips

for the marinade

1 tbsp soy sauce
1 tbsp honey
1/2 tsp Chinese five-spice powder

Score the fat on the duck breasts in a lattice pattern and rub with salt. For the marinade, mix the soy sauce, honey and five-spice powder, and spoon this over the flesh side of the duck. Marinate in the fridge for at least 1 hour.

Remove the duck from the marinade and pat dry. Heat a non-stick pan and add the duck, fat down. Cook for about 10 minutes, then pour off most of the fat and turn the duck. Fry for a further 5 minutes, until cooked through. Transfer to a board and leave to rest for 5 minutes.

Spread each pancake with a thin layer of hoisin sauce. Slice the duck thinly, then place a couple of slices of duck on each pancake, top with a little spring onion and a few sticks of cucumber and fold into a cone. Repeat with the remaining ingredients and serve.

Serves 4

sticky glazed pork ribs

see variations page 200

Serve these sticky ribs to chew on with drinks or arrange them on salad leaves for a sit-down appetizer, either way, be sure you offer plenty of napkins for wiping sticky fingers.

3 tbsp clear honey
1 tsp soy sauce
2 tsp Chinese five-spice powder

Ground black pepper
12 pork ribs

Preheat the oven to 200°C/400°G/Gas Mark 6.

Combine the honey, soy sauce and five-spice powder, and season with black pepper in a large bowl. Add the ribs and turn them to coat them all over in the honey mixture.

Put the ribs in a roasting pan in a single layer, scraping all the glaze over them, and bake for 30 minutes, until glossy and well browned. Serve hot.

Serves 4

pea & potato pakora with yogurt

see variations page 201

These crisp and spicy little battered bites are delicious with plain yogurt for dunking.
Serve them as a snack with drinks, or with a selection of Asian-style dips and relishes.

450 g/1 lb potatoes, boiled and mashed
125 g/4¹/₂ oz frozen peas, thawed
2–3 fresh green chillies, seeded and finely
    chopped
4 spring onions, finely sliced
2 tsp ground cumin
1 tsp ground coriander
3 tbsp chopped fresh coriander leaves

115 g/4 oz gram flour (chickpea flour or besan)
¹/₂ tsp chilli powder
1 tsp ground turmeric
1 tsp baking powder
200 ml/7 fl oz cold water
Sunflower oil, for deep-frying
Salt
Plain yogurt, to serve

Mix the potatoes, peas, chillies, spring onions, cumin, ground and fresh coriander. Season
with salt and stir to combine. Shape into 16 walnut-sized balls, place on a platter and chill
for at least 30 minutes, until firm.

Mix the gram flour, chilli, turmeric and baking powder in a bowl. Using a fork, stir in a
quarter of the water to make a thick, smooth paste. Stir in the remaining water smoothly.

Heat the oil for frying to 180°C/350°F, or until a cube of bread browns in about 1 minute.
Dip the balls in the batter and fry for about 2 minutes, until golden. Remove with a slotted
spoon and drain on kitchen paper. Keep hot until all are ready. Serve with yogurt for dipping.

Serves 4

variations

thai crab cakes with chilli vinegar

see base recipe page 177

green curry crab cakes
Prepare the basic recipe, using green curry paste in place of the red curry paste.

thai crab cakes with lemon grass
Finely chop the fleshy bulb of 1 lemon grass stalk. Prepare the basic recipe, adding the chopped lemon grass to the crab cake mixture.

zesty thai crab cakes
Prepare the basic recipe, adding the grated rind of 1 lime to the crab cake mixture.

thai crab cakes with sweet chilli sauce
Prepare the basic recipe and serve the crab cakes with sweet chilli sauce in place of the chilli vinegar.

variations

chicken satay with spicy peanut sauce

see base recipe page 179

pork satay
Prepare the basic recipe, using strips of pork loin in place of the chicken.

beef satay
Prepare the basic recipe, using strips of beef fillet in place of the chicken.

tofu satay
Prepare the basic recipe, using fingers of firm tofu in place of the chicken.

prawn satay
Prepare the basic recipe, using peeled raw tiger prawns in place of the
chicken. Allow 2 prawns per skewer.

salt & pepper squid

see base recipe page 180

hot chilli squid
Prepare the basic recipe, using 1 teaspoon dried chilli flakes in place of the black pepper.

spiced salt & pepper squid
Prepare the basic recipe, adding 1 teaspoon ground cumin to the salt and pepper mixture.

salt & pepper squid with coriander
Prepare the basic recipe, sprinkling the fried squid with chopped fresh coriander leaves before serving.

salt & pepper squid with lemon
Prepare the basic recipe, using lemons in place of the limes.

variations

fruity lamb samosas

see base recipe page 183

spicy beef samosas
Prepare the basic recipe, using minced beef in place of the lamb, and omitting the mango chutney.

spicy chicken samosas
Prepare the basic recipe, using minced chicken in place of the lamb.

spicy pork samosas
Prepare the basic recipe, using minced pork in place of the lamb.

spicy lamb & pea samosas
Prepare the basic recipe, adding 50 g/1³/4 oz thawed frozen peas to the lamb mixture.

spicy lamb samosas with coriander
Prepare the basic recipe, adding 3 tablespoons chopped fresh coriander to the lamb mixture.

variations

sushi rolls

see base recipe page 184

roast pepper & crab sushi rolls
Prepare the basic recipe, using strips of roast pepper in place of the cucumber.

avocado & smoked salmon sushi
Prepare the basic recipe, using strips of smoked salmon and mashed avocado in place of the crab mix and cucumber.

egg-cup sushi
Prepare the basic recipe for sushi rice. Line an egg cup with clear film, then press a thin slice of smoked salmon in it. Fill with rice, then turn out. Repeat to make more sushi moulds.

tuna & cucumber sushi
Prepare the basic recipe, using tuna in place of the crab meat.

roast pepper & avocado sushi
Prepare the basic recipe, using mashed avocado spiked with wasabi in place of the crab, and strips of roast red pepper in place of the cucumber.

variations

vietnamese crystal rolls

see base recipe page 187

vietnamese crystal rolls with avocado
Finely dice the flesh of 1 avocado and sprinkle over the beansprouts with the other filling ingredients.

vietnamese crystal rolls with sweet pepper
Finely dice 1 red or yellow pepper and sprinkle over the beansprouts with the other filling ingredients.

vietnamese crystal rolls with chicken
Skin and dice 1 cooked boneless chicken breast and use in place of the tofu.

vietnamese crystal rolls with basil
Prepare the basic recipe, using chopped fresh basil in place of the coriander.

vietnamese crystal rolls with mint
Prepare the basic recipe, using chopped fresh mint in place of the coriander.

variations

peking duck wraps

see base recipe page 188

sweet & spicy duck wraps
Prepare the basic recipe, spreading the pancakes with sweet chilli sauce instead of hoisin sauce.

duck wraps with fresh mango
Cut the flesh of $^1/_2$ peeled and stoned mango into matchstick strips. Prepare the basic recipe, adding a few sticks of mango to each wrap.

gingered duck wraps
Prepare the basic recipe, adding 1 teaspoon grated fresh root ginger to the duck marinade.

garlic-marinated duck wraps
Prepare the basic recipe, stirring 1 crushed garlic clove into the marinade.

duck wraps with beansprouts
Prepare the basic recipe, adding a few beansprouts to each filled pancake before rolling up.

variations

sticky glazed pork ribs

see base recipe page 191

spicy glazed pork ribs
Prepare the basic recipe, adding ¹/₄ teaspoon crushed dried chilli to the honey and soy mixture.

sticky glazed pork ribs with ginger
Prepare the basic recipe, adding 1 teaspoon grated fresh root ginger to the honey and soy mixture.

sticky glazed pork ribs with cinnamon
Prepare the basic recipe, adding 1 teaspoon ground cinnamon to the honey and soy mixture.

sticky glazed pork ribs with cumin
Prepare the basic recipe, adding 1 teaspoon ground cumin to the honey and soy mixture.

variations

pea & potato pakora with yogurt

see base recipe page 192

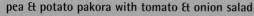

pea & potato pakora with tomato & onion salad
Finely slice 1 red onion and dice 4 seeded tomatoes. Season with salt and pepper, squeeze the juice of 1 lime over and serve with the pakora.

minty pea & potato pakoras
Prepare the basic recipe, using 1$^{1}/_{2}$ tablespoons chopped fresh mint in place of the fresh coriander.

pea & potato pakoras with mango chutney
Prepare the basic recipe and serve with mango chutney.

pea & potato pakora with minted yogurt
Stir 3 tablespoons chopped fresh mint into 235 ml/8 fl oz plain yogurt and season with a pinch of salt and a pinch of cayenne pepper. Serve with the pakora.

quick canapés & hors d'oeuvres

These elegant starters are fast, easy and delicious.

Less time in the kitchen means more time to be

with your guests – but no-one will think you've

scrimped on time when you produce a platter of

these elegant bites.

hummus & roast pepper
mini wraps

see variations page 219

You can rustle up these pretty tortilla pinwheels in less than 10 minutes – making them the perfect choice for instant entertaining.

2 soft flour tortillas
6 tbsp hummus

2 bottled roast red peppers
Ground black pepper

Lay the tortillas on a board and spread each one with 3 tablespoons hummus.

Pat the peppers dry on kitchen paper, then cut into strips and scatter over the tortillas. Season with black pepper and roll up the tortillas tightly. Trim off the ends of each roll and slice each roll into six pieces. Arrange the mini wraps on a serving plate.

Makes 12

mini blinis with horseradish cream & caviar

see variations page 220

You can buy packets of blinis from most good supermarkets. Serve them cold if you want to prepare these canapés ahead, but they're even better warm.

12 mini blinis
6 tbsp crème fraîche or sour cream
$3/4$ tsp grated lemon rind

$3/4$ tsp creamed horseradish
1–2 tbsp caviar
Snipped fresh chives, for sprinkling (optional)

Preheat the oven according to the packet instructions for heating the blini. Combine the crème fraîche or sour cream with the lemon rind and horseradish and set aside.

Arrange the blinis on a baking sheet and warm through for about 5 minutes or according to the packet instructions. Then arrange the blinis on a serving platter.

Top each blini with a spoonful of the crème fraîche or sour cream mixture and about $1/4$ teaspoon caviar. Sprinkle with snipped chives and serve.

Makes 12

smashed pea & ham crostini

see variations page 221

Buy a very elegant, narrow baguette to make these crostini. If you can only find larger baguettes, cut the slices in half to make bite-size toasts.

2 shallots, finely chopped
2 tbsp olive oil, plus extra for drizzling
140 g/5 oz frozen peas
2 tbsp white wine
3 strips prosciutto

12 thin baguette slices
1 garlic clove, halved
Chopped fresh mint, for sprinkling
Salt and ground black pepper

Gently fry the shallots in the oil for about 3 minutes, until slightly softened. Add the peas and wine, cover and cook gently for about 4 minutes, until the peas are tender.

Meanwhile, cut each strip of prosciutto in half widthways, then across to make twelve strips. Turn the peas and juices into a food processor, season with salt and pepper and process to make a chunky purée.

Preheat the grill. Toast the bread on both sides until golden. Rub one side of each toast with the cut side of the garlic clove, then spoon smashed peas on top and finish with a twist of ham. Drizzle with a little more oil, if liked, and a grinding of black pepper.

Sprinkle the crostini with mint and serve immediately.

Makes 12

mini poppadums with onion relish

see variations page 222

Simple, light and refreshing, these elegant appetisers are great with cocktails. For a more informal approach, serve the relish in a bowl and the poppadoms for scooping.

1 red onion, quartered and thinly sliced
$1/4$ cucumber, halved, seeded and sliced
1 green chilli, seeded and finely chopped
$1/4$ tsp ground coriander
Handful of fresh coriander leaves, chopped

Pinch of sugar
Juice of 1 lime
16 mini poppadums
Salt and ground black pepper

Put the onion, cucumber and chilli in a bowl. Sprinkle over the ground and fresh coriander and sugar and season with salt, then squeeze the lime juice over. Toss to combine.

Arrange the mini poppadums on a plate and fill each one with a spoonful of the onion relish. Serve immediately.

Makes 16

pesto & artichoke bruschetta

see variations page 223

Nothing could be simpler than these bruschetta. There are all kinds of char-grilled, marinated artichokes available, so select the type you prefer.

2 tbsp pesto
2 tbsp crème fraîche
12 thin baguette slices
12 fresh basil leaves

Small jar of char-grilled artichoke hearts,
    drained (12 pieces)
Ground black pepper

Combine the pesto and crème fraîche, then set aside.

Preheat the grill and toast the bread until golden on both sides. Spread each toast with pesto mixture, top with a piece of artichoke heart and add a fresh basil leaf. Serve freshly prepared.

Makes 12

walnut toasts with warm goat's cheese & fig

see variations page 224

Tart, piquant goat's cheese and sweet juicy fig are a natural partnership for a simple, elegant canapé on rich walnut toast.

4 slices walnut bread
115 g/4 oz goat's cheese

2 tbsp toasted pine nuts
2 fresh figs, each cut into 6 wedges

Preheat the grill. Cut each slice of bread into three bite-size pieces and toast on one side.

Meanwhile, slice the goat's cheese and cut it into 12 bite-size pieces. Turn the toasts, uncooked sides up. Top each toast with a piece of cheese and grill for about 2 minutes, until golden and bubbling.

Sprinkle the pine nuts over the toasts, top with a wedge of fig and serve immediately.

Makes 12

pumpernickel with sour cream & beetroot caviar

see variations page 225

The distinctive taste of dark brown pumpernickel is sublime with sour cream and sweet, juicy beetroot in these Eastern-European canapés.

1 tsp balsamic vinegar
1 tsp olive oil
$^1/_4$–$^1/_2$ tsp wholegrain mustard
2 cooked beetroot, finely diced

4 slices pumpernickel, rye bread or stoneground
    wholemeal bread
120 ml/4 fl oz sour cream
Snipped fresh chives, to garnish

Mix the vinegar, oil and mustard together in a large bowl. Add the beetroot and toss it with the dressing.

Cut each slice of pumpernickel into four squares and arrange them on a serving platter. Top each slice with a dollop of sour cream, a spoonful of beetroot and a sprinkling of chives. Serve freshly prepared.

Serves 4

smoked mackerel pâté on finger toasts

see variations page 226

As a snack with drinks, this quick appetizer couldn't be simpler and it can be served with salad as a more formal starter. Leftover pâté can be stored in a covered container in the refrigerator for 3 to 4 days.

200 g/7 oz smoked mackerel fillets, skinned
120 ml/4 fl oz Greek yogurt
Juice of 1/4 to 1/2 lemon

4 slices wholegrain bread
Chopped fresh parsley, for sprinkling
Ground black pepper

Put the fish and yogurt in a food processor, season with black pepper and process to a smooth pâté. Stir in lemon juice to taste.

Remove the crusts from the bread, then toast the slices on both sides. Slice each toast into 3 fingers, spread with pâté, sprinkle with chopped fresh parsley and serve.

Serves 4

crostini with blue cheese & pear

see variations page 227

Sharp, salty blue cheese and sweet, juicy pear make a sublime combination on these crunchy little toasts. Creamy gorgonzola is particularly good, but any blue cheese will do.

1 pear
12 thin baguette slices

75 g/2³/₄ oz gorgonzola cheese, thinly sliced
Freshly ground black pepper

Peel and core the pear, then slice it into 12 thin wedges.

Preheat the grill and toast the bread until golden on both sides. Top each toast with a sliver of blue cheese, a wedge of pear and a good grinding of black pepper. Serve immediately.

Makes 12

variations

hummus & roast pepper mini wraps

see base recipe page 203

hummus, roast pepper & basil mini wraps

Prepare the basic recipe, scattering a few fresh basil leaves over the peppers before rolling up and slicing.

hummus, roast pepper & sweet chilli mini wraps

Prepare the basic recipe, drizzling 1 teaspoon sweet chilli sauce over each hummus-spread wrap before scattering the peppers over and rolling up.

cream cheese & red pepper mini wraps

Prepare the basic recipe, using cream cheese in place of the hummus.

cream cheese & smoked salmon mini wraps

Cut 55 g/2 oz smoked salmon into strips. Prepare the basic recipe using cream cheese in place of the hummus, and scattering the wraps with the smoked salmon in place of the red pepper.

hummus, carrot & coriander mini wraps

Peel and grate 1 carrot and chop a handful of fresh coriander leaves. Prepare the basic recipe, scattering grated carrot over the hummus in place of the red pepper, and sprinkling with coriander before rolling up.

variations

mini blinis with horseradish cream & caviar

see base recipe page 205

mini blinis with horseradish cream & roast pepper strips
Prepare the basic recipe, using strips of bottled roast pepper in place of the caviar.

mini blinis with horseradish cream & salami twists
Prepare the basic recipe, using strips of salami in place of the caviar.

mini blinis with horseradish cream & smoked trout
Gently break a smoked trout fillet into 12 flakes, removing any bones. Prepare the basic recipe, using the smoked trout in place of the caviar.

mini blinis with smoked salmon
Prepare the basic recipe, topping each blini with a strip of smoked salmon in place of the caviar.

mini blinis with smoked salmon & caviar
Prepare the basic recipe, topping each blini with a strip of smoked salmon and a dollop of caviar .

variations

smashed pea & ham crostini

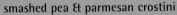
see base recipe page 206

smashed pea & parmesan crostini
Prepare the basic recipe, topping each crostini with shavings of Parmesan cheese in place of the prosciutto.

smashed pea & smoked trout crostini
Gently break a smoked trout fillet into 12 large flakes. Prepare the basic recipe, topping each crostini with a piece of smoked trout in place of the prosciutto.

smashed pea & cherry tomato crostini
Cut 12 cherry tomatoes in half. Prepare the basic recipe, topping each crostini with 2 cherry tomato halves in place of the prosciutto.

smashed pea & chorizo crostini
Prepare the basic recipe, using 12 slices of wafer-thin chorizo in place of the prosciutto.

smashed pea crostini with sun-dried tomatoes
Drain 4 sun-dried tomatoes in oil, then slice thinly. Prepare the basic recipe, topping the crostini with strips of sun-dried tomato in place of the prosciutto.

variations

mini poppadums with onion relish

see base recipe page 209

mini poppadums with onion & tomato relish
Prepare the basic recipe, adding 1 finely chopped, seeded tomato to the relish.

mini poppadums with onion & mango relish
Prepare the basic recipe, adding 1/2 small chopped, peeled and stoned mango to the relish in place of the cucumber.

mini poppadums with onion & coconut relish
Prepare the basic recipe, adding 2 tablespoons grated fresh coconut to the onion relish.

mini poppadums with onion relish & mango chutney
Prepare the basic recipe, adding a dollop of mango chutney to each relish-filled poppadum.

pesto & artichoke bruschetta

see base recipe page 210

garlic & artichoke bruschetta
Halve a garlic clove. Prepare the basic recipe, rubbing the toasts with garlic and drizzling them with a little extra virgin olive oil instead of spreading with pesto.

pesto & artichoke bruschetta with rocket
Prepare the basic recipe, adding a few rocket leaves to each bruschetta in place of the basil leaves.

pesto & artichoke bruschetta with olives
Prepare the basic recipe, adding a pitted black or stuffed green olive to each bruschetta.

pesto & artichoke bruschetta with pecorino
Prepare the basic recipe, adding a few shavings of pecorino to top off each bruschetta.

pesto & cherry tomato bruschetta
Prepare the basic recipe, topping each toast with 3 cherry tomato halves.

variations

walnut toasts with warm goat's cheese & fig

see base recipe page 213

bruschetta with warm goat's cheese & fig
Prepare the basic recipe, using 12 baguette slices in place of the walnut bread. Toast on both sides until golden, then simply top with the cheese, a wedge of fig and a grinding of black pepper.

walnut toasts with goat's cheese & chilli jam
Prepare the basic recipe, spreading the toast with chilli jam before topping with goat's cheese.

walnut toasts with goat's cheese & peach
Prepare the basic recipe, using a ripe peach cut into slim wedges in place of the figs.

walnut toasts with goat's cheese & honey
Prepare the basic recipe, drizzling the goat's cheese with a little clear honey before grilling.

variations

pumpernickel with sour cream & beetroot caviar

see base recipe page 214

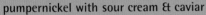

pumpernickel with sour cream & caviar
Prepare the basic recipe, topping each canapé with a teaspoonful of caviar
in place of the dressed beetroot.

pumpernickel with sour cream & char-grilled artichokes
Drain a bottle of marinated artichoke hearts and, if necessary, cut in half,
Prepare the basic recipe, using the artichoke hearts in place of the dressed
beetroot. Sprinkle with grated lemon rind and a grinding of black pepper.

pumpernickel with sour cream & smoked salmon
Cut 1 to 2 slices of smoked salmon into 12 strips. Prepare the basic recipe,
adding a twist of smoked salmon in place of the dressed beetroot.

pumpernickel with sour cream & pickled herrings
Drain 12 pickled herrings. Prepare the basic recipe, topping each canapé with
a pickled herring in place of the dressed beetroot.

pumpernickel with sour cream & roast peppers
Drain 3 bottled roast peppers, pat dry on kitchen paper, then slice each into
quarters. Prepare the basic recipe using roast pepper in place of beetroot.

variations

smoked mackerel pâté on finger toasts

see base recipe page 217

smoked trout pâté
Prepare the basic recipe using smoked trout in place of smoked mackerel.

smoked mackerel pâté on toasted pitta
Prepare the basic recipe, using pitta bread instead of wholegrain bread, and slicing them across into fingers.

smoked mackerel pâté on pumpernickel squares
Prepare the basic recipe and serve with squares of pumpernickel in place of the finger toasts.

smoked mackerel pâté on baguette toasts
Prepare the basic recipe, using 12 thin slices of baguette in place of the wholegrain bread.

smoked mackerel pâté with cherry tomatoes
Prepare the basic recipe, spreading the pâté on the toasts and topping with halved cherry tomatoes.

crostini with blue cheese & pear

see base recipe page 218

crostini with blue cheese, pear & pecan nuts
Prepare the basic recipe, topping each crostini with a pecan half.

crostini with blue cheese, pear & rocket
Prepare the basic recipe, topping each crostini with a couple of rocket leaves.

crostini with blue cheese, pear & honey
Prepare the basic recipe, drizzling about $1/4$ teaspoon clear honey over each
finished crostini.

crostini with blue cheese, pear & watercress
Prepare the basic recipe, topping each crostini with a sprig of watercress.

crostini with pear & pecorino
Prepare the basic recipe, using shavings of pecorino in place of the
gorgonzola.

mouthwatering salads

Light, fresh and zingy, crisp and crunchy ... salads are the ideal way to tease the tasebuds without spoiling your appetite. Serve them before a simple supper or for a sophisticated dinner – they are perfect for either.

fennel & orange salad

see variations page 245

This light, refreshing, low-fat salad is perfect for whetting the appetite, at the same time leaving plenty of room for the main course.

2 fennel bulbs
Juice of $^1/_2$ lemon
3 oranges

Handful of black olives
Salt and ground black pepper

Finely slice the fennel and place it in a bowl. Squeeze the lemon juice over and toss to combine.

Cut away the peel from the oranges. Holding the fruit over the fennel, cut between the membranes to remove the segments and add them to the fennel. Squeeze any juice from the membranes over the fennel before discarding the membranes.

Add the olives to the salad, season with salt and pepper, and toss to combine. Divide among four plates and serve immediately.

Serves 4

roast pepper salad with mint & pumpkin seeds

see variations page 246

Roasting peppers really brings out their sweet, intense smoky flavour. This salad is great for entertaining because it can be prepared in advance, then plated just before serving.

2 red peppers
2 yellow peppers
2 tbsp pumpkin seeds
2 tsp red wine vinegar

$1/4$ tsp Dijon mustard
2 tbsp olive oil
2 tsp chopped fresh mint
Salt and ground black pepper

Preheat the oven to 230°C/450°F/Gas Mark 8. Roast the peppers on a baking sheet for about 40 minutes, until blackened. Transfer to a bowl, cover with clear film and leave to cool.

Meanwhile, heat a dry frying pan, add the pumpkin seeds and toast for 3 to 4 minutes, shaking the pan occasionally, until golden. Set aside.

In a large bowl, whisk together the vinegar, mustard, oil and mint, and season with salt and pepper. Peel and seed the peppers, then cut the flesh into strips. Add the strips to the dressing and toss to combine. Cover and leave to stand for about 30 minutes.

Divide the peppers among four plates, sprinkle with pumpkin seeds and serve.

Serves 4

char-grilled courgette salad with feta, mint & lemon

see variations page 247

The combination of sweet, smoky and tender char-grilled courgettes, salty feta and fresh, zingy lemon is quite divine. Make it in the summer when courgettes are in season.

1 tbsp lemon juice
Pinch of sugar
4 tbsp olive oil, plus extra for brushing
2 tsp chopped fresh mint

3 courgettes
115 g/4 oz feta cheese, crumbled
Salt and ground black pepper

Whisk together the lemon juice, sugar, olive oil and mint. Set aside.

Preheat a griddle pan. Slice the courgettes on the diagonal into 7 mm/1/4 in thick slices. Brush with oil, then press the slices on to the griddle pan and cook for about 4 minutes on each side, until tender and charred.

Arrange the courgettes on four plates, sprinkle the feta over them and drizzle with dressing. Serve freshly dressed.

Serves 4

beetroot, halloumi & green bean salad

see variations page 248

Sweet, juicy beetroot; warm, salty halloumi; and crisp, fresh green beans are a fabulous combination in this simple summer salad.

1²/₃ tsp lemon juice
¹/₂ tsp grated lemon rind
¹/₄ tsp honey
Good pinch of dried chilli flakes
2 tbsp olive oil

Salt
200 g/7 oz green beans
250 g/9 oz cooked beetroot
250 g/9 oz halloumi, sliced into 1 cm/¹/₂ in
    thick slices

Whisk the lemon juice and rind, honey, chilli and olive oil with a pinch of salt and set aside.

Cook the beans for about 4 minutes in boiling water, until just tender, then drain and refresh under cold water. Slice the beetroot, then cut the slices in the opposite direction to make matchstick strips and place in a bowl. Add the beans to the beetroot. Drizzle the dressing over and toss to combine.

Preheat a griddle, then cook the halloumi for about 2 minutes on each side until charred.

Divide the salad among four plates, top with slices of halloumi and serve at once.

Serves 4

duck & pomegranate salad

see variations page 249

The easiest way to remove the seeds from a pomegranate is to cut the fruit in half, hold it over a bowl and bash the back with a wooden spoon. The seeds will simply pop out.

2 duck breasts
1 tbsp red wine vinegar
$1/2$ tsp Dijon mustard
Pinch of sugar
2 tbsp olive oil

Salt and ground black pepper
2 handfuls watercress
2 handfuls rocket
Seeds of 1 pomegranate

Score the skin on the duck in a lattice pattern and rub with salt. Heat a non-stick frying pan. Place the duck in the pan, skin side down, and cook for 10 minutes. Pour away most of the fat, turn the duck over and cook for another 4 to 5 minutes. Transfer the duck to a board, cover with foil and leave to rest.

Meanwhile, whisk together the vinegar, mustard, sugar and olive oil and season to taste with black pepper.

Divide the salad leaves among four plates. Slice the duck breasts and scatter the slices over the leaves. Sprinkle with the pomegranate seeds, drizzle with dressing and serve.

Serves 4

fig & prosciutto salad

see variations page 250

Sweet, juicy figs and salty, wafer-thin slices of prosciutto are a classic combination – and nowhere better than in this simple, luscious salad.

1 tbsp balsamic vinegar
2 tbsp olive oil
Salt and ground black pepper
1 spring onion, finely chopped

4 handfuls mixed salad leaves (about 115 g/4 oz)
4 figs
8 slices prosciutto

Whisk together the vinegar and oil with seasoning. Divide the salad leaves among four plates. Cut the figs into wedges, then scatter these over the salads. Tear the prosciutto into bite-size pieces and scatter them over the salads.

Drizzle the dressing over the salads and serve.

Serves 4

mango & seared beef salad with wasabi dressing

see variations page 251

Sweet, juicy mango and tender seared beef make a sublime combination in this refreshing salad. Wasabi, the pale green Japanese mustard, is very peppery (like a fiery horseradish), so add more or less according to taste.

2 sirloin steaks
3 tbsp sunflower oil, plus extra for brushing
1 tbsp red wine vinegar
$^1/_2$ to 1 tsp wasabi
Pinch of sugar

Salt
4 handfuls watercress
1 red onion, thinly sliced
1 mango, peeled and pitted

Preheat a griddle pan. Brush the steaks with some of the oil and season, then cook for 3 to 4 minutes on each side, until medium rare. Set aside.

Whisk together the remaining oil, red wine vinegar, wasabi and sugar, and season to taste.

Put a handful of watercress on each plate, then scatter the onion over the top. Cut the mango into bite-size pieces and scatter them over the salad. Slice the steaks and divide the slices among the plates, then drizzle with the dressing and serve.

Serves 4

baby spinach, roast squash & gorgonzola salad

see variations page 252

Roasting brings out the intense, sweet flavour of the squash and the heat helps to melt the gorgonzola and wilt the spinach leaves to create a deliciously different salad.

1 small butternut squash
1 1/2 tbsp olive oil, plus extra for drizzling
Salt and ground black pepper
1 tbsp balsamic vinegar

1/2 tsp wholegrain mustard
115 g/4 oz baby spinach
100 g/3 1/2 oz gorgonzola or other blue cheese, cut into slices or crumbled

Preheat the oven to 200°C/400°F/Gas Mark 6. Halve, seed and peel the squash, then slice it into twelve wedges and put in a baking dish or roasting pan. Drizzle with oil, season and turn the wedges to coat them with oil all over. Roast for about 20 minutes, until tender.

Meanwhile, whisk together the oil, vinegar and mustard and set aside.

Divide the spinach leaves among four plates or salad bowls. Scatter the cheese over them. Add three wedges of squash to each salad, drizzle with dressing and serve immediately.

Serves 4

avocado & grapefruit salad

see variations page 253

The combination of sweet yet zingy grapefruit and creamy avocado is the perfect way to make the mouth water in anticipation of the meal to follow. This salad takes only minutes to prepare and it looks stunning.

2 tsp raspberry vinegar
1 tsp Dijon mustard
Good pinch of sugar
1 1/2 tbsp olive oil
Ground black pepper

85 g/3 oz mixed leaves, such as spinach, rocket
    and watercress
2 ruby grapefruit
2 avocados

Whisk together the vinegar, mustard, sugar and oil, season with black pepper and set aside.

Put the salad leaves in a bowl. Cut away the peel from the grapefruit, then cut between the membranes to remove the segments, reserving any juice. Add the fruit to the salad and drizzle the reserved juices over it.

Peel and pit the avocados, then cut the flesh into bite-size pieces and add these to the salad. Drizzle with the dressing and toss to combine all the ingredients with the dressing.

Arrange the salad on individual plates, drizzling over the dressing, and serve immediately.

Serves 4

fennel & orange salad

see base recipe page 229

fennel, orange & char-grilled spring onion salad
Prepare the basic recipe. Trim 2 bunches of spring onions, brush with oil, then grill for 2 to 3 minutes on each side until tender. Add to the salad and serve.

fennel, orange & red onion salad
Prepare the basic recipe, adding $1/2$ finely sliced red onion to the salad.

fennel & orange salad with mint
Prepare the basic recipe, sprinkling the salad with 2 teaspoons chopped fresh mint.

fennel & orange salad with chives
Prepare the basic recipe, sprinkling the salad with 1 tablespoon snipped fresh chives.

variations

roast pepper salad with mint & pumpkin seeds

see base recipe page 231

roast pepper & anchovy salad
Prepare the basic recipe, adding 8 anchovy fillets, halved lengthways. Omit the salt from the dressing as the anchovies are salty.

roast pepper salad with toasted pine nuts
Prepare the basic recipe, using toasted pine nuts instead of pumpkin seeds.

roast pepper & tomato salad
Prepare the basic recipe, adding 4 chopped, seeded and peeled tomatoes to the salad.

roast pepper salad with capers
Prepare the basic recipe, adding 1 teaspoon chopped, rinsed capers to the dressing. Omit the salt from the dressing as the capers are salty.

roast pepper & rocket salad
Prepare the basic recipe and serve each salad on a handful of rocket leaves.

char-grilled courgette salad with feta, mint & lemon

see base recipe page 232

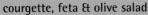

courgette, feta & olive salad
Prepare the basic recipe, adding 4 or 5 black olives to each salad.

char-grilled courgette & pepper salad with feta
Seed two red peppers and cut them into eighths. Prepare the basic recipe using 1^1/$_2$ courgettes and grilling the pieces of pepper at the same time as the courgette slices.

pasta salad with char-grilled courgettes & feta
Cook 115 g/4 oz fusilli according to the instructions on the packet. Drain and set aside. Prepare the basic recipe using 2 courgettes. Toss the courgettes, feta and dressing with the pasta and divide among plates.

fiery courgette & feta salad
Prepare the basic recipe, adding 1 finely chopped, seeded fresh red chilli to the dressing.

variations

beetroot, halloumi & green bean salad

see base recipe page 235

beetroot, halloumi & green bean salad with black olives
Prepare the basic recipe, tossing a handful of black olives into the salad.

beetroot, halloumi and green bean salad with red onion
Prepare the basic recipe, tossing $1/2$ finely sliced red onion into the salad.

beetroot, halloumi & sugar snap salad
Prepare the basic recipe, using sugar snap peas in place of the green beans.

beetroot, halloumi & green bean salad with mint dressing
Prepare the basic recipe, adding 1 teaspoon chopped fresh mint to the dressing.

beetroot, halloumi & green bean salad with orange
Cut away the peel from an orange, then slice between the membranes to remove the segments. Prepare the basic recipe, adding the orange segments to the salad.

variations

duck & pomegranate salad

see base recipe page 236

fragrant duck & pomegranate salad
Prepare the basic recipe, adding a handful of fragrant herb leaves, such as coriander, basil and mint, to the salad leaves.

duck, orange & pomegranate salad
Cut away the peel from an orange, then slice between the membranes to remove the segments. Prepare the basic recipe, adding the orange segments to the salad leaves.

duck & pomegranate salad with mild leaves
Prepare the basic recipe, using lamb's lettuce and baby spinach leaves in place of the watercress and rocket.

duck & pomegranate salad with red onion
Prepare the basic recipe, sprinkling the salad leaves with $1/2$ finely sliced red onion.

variations

fig & prosciutto salad

see base recipe page 239

nectarine & prosciutto salad
Prepare the basic recipe, using 2 stoned nectarines in place of the figs.

fig & parmesan salad
Prepare the basic recipe, scattering the salad with parmesan shavings in place of the prosciutto.

fig & prosciutto salad with roast chillies
Prepare the basic recipe, scattering the salads with 2 finely chopped, bottled roast chillies.

fig & ricotta salad
Prepare the basic recipe, spooning a couple of tablespoonfuls of ricotta cheese over each salad in place of the prosciutto.

fig, prosciutto & watercress salad
Prepare the basic recipe, using watercress in place of the mixed salad leaves.

mango & seared beef salad with wasabi dressing

see base recipe page 240

mango, cucumber & seared beef salad with wasabi dressing
Prepare the basic recipe, tossing $1/2$ small sliced cucumber into the salad with the mango and onion.

mango, coriander & seared beef salad with wasabi dressing
Prepare the basic recipe, adding a handful of fresh coriander leaves to the watercress.

kiwi & seared beef salad with wasabi dressing
Prepare the basic recipe, using 3 peeled kiwi fruit in place of the mango.

blueberry & seared beef salad with wasabi dressing
Prepare the basic recipe, using a handful of blueberries instead of mango.

mango & chicken salad with wasabi dressing
Prepare the basic recipe, using 2 grilled chicken breasts in place of the seared steaks.

variations

baby spinach, roast squash & gorgonzola salad

see base recipe page 243

baby spinach, new potato & gorgonzola salad
Prepare the basic recipe, using hot, freshly boiled new potatoes in place of the butternut squash.

baby spinach, roast squash & feta salad
Prepare the basic recipe, using crumbled feta in place of the gorgonzola.

baby spinach, roast squash & gorgonzola salad with toasted pine nuts
Prepare the basic recipe, sprinkling 2 tablespoon toasted pine nuts over the salad.

baby spinach, roast beetroot & gorgonzola salad
Prepare the basic recipe, using 3 cooked beetroots in place of the butternut squash. Peel the beetroots and cut into wedges, then drizzle with oil, season and roast in the same way.

baby spinach, roast jerusalem artichokes & gorgonzola salad
Prepare the basic recipe, using Jerusalem artichokes instead of squash. Peel the artichokes, then boil in lightly salted water for about 10 minutes, until almost tender. Put 1 tablespoon olive oil in a roasting pan and place in the oven for 5 minutes. Add the artichokes, toss to coat, then roast until golden.

variations

avocado & grapefruit salad

see base recipe page 244

chicken, avocado & grapefruit salad
Prepare the basic recipe, adding 2 sliced, grilled chicken breasts to the salad.

mozzarella, avocado & grapefruit salad
Prepare the basic recipe, adding four or five bocconcini (baby mozzarella) to each portion of salad.

prawn, avocado & grapefruit salad
Prepare the basic recipe, adding 200 g/7 oz peeled cooked prawns to the salad.

avocado, grapefruit & spring onion salad
Prepare the basic recipe, adding 1 bunch sliced spring onions to the salad.

avocado, grapefruit & hazelnut salad
Prepare the basic recipe, and scatter 2 tablespoons of chopped toasted hazelnuts over the top.

elegant starters

From soups and tarts to more-ish shellfish and

creamy pâtés that are perfect year-round,

these appetisers kickstart the tastebuds and set

the stage for a dramatic second act.

vichyssoise with sour cream & chives

see variations page 274

This smooth, creamy chilled soup makes an elegant appetiser for a sophisticated dinner. It's a great classic for entertaining because you can prepare it in advance.

2 tbsp olive oil
1 onion, chopped
3 large leeks, sliced
1 potato, peeled and cut into chunks
750 ml/24 fl oz vegetable stock

200 ml/7 fl oz milk
200 ml/7 fl oz single cream
Juice of $1/2$ lemon
Salt and ground black pepper
Sour cream and snipped fresh chives, to garnish

Heat the oil in a pan, then fry the onion and leeks for about 5 minutes, until tender. Add the potato chunks and stock. Bring to the boil, reduce the heat and cover. Simmer for about 15 minutes, until the potatoes are tender.

Blend the soup until smooth in a food processor or blender. Stir in the milk, cream and lemon juice, and season to taste. Leave the soup to cool, then chill it for at least 2 hours.

The soup will thicken on standing, so add a splash more milk if needed before serving. Check the seasoning, squeeze in a little more lemon juice, if needed, and serve with a swirl of sour cream and a sprinkling of chives.

Serves 4

marinated seared scallops

see variations page 275

Quick and simple, yet sophisticated and utterly delicious, these scallops are the perfect way to start a dinner party. For hungry diners, add one or two extra scallops per person.

12 large scallops
1 fresh red chilli, seeded and chopped
Grated rind and juice of 1 lime

2 tsp chopped fresh mint
1 tbsp olive oil
Salt

Put the scallops in a dish in a single layer. Whisk together the chilli, lime rind and juice, mint and olive oil with a pinch of salt. Pour over the scallops, turning them to coat them evenly.

Heat a non-stick frying pan. Add the scallops and their dressing and cook for about 1 minute on each side, until just cooked through. Serve immediately, drizzled with the juices.

Serves 4

filo tartlets with cherry tomatoes, basil & ricotta

see variations page 276

These crisp, golden tartlets filled with baked ricotta and garlic-flavoured tomatoes make an elegant start to a special meal.

8 sheets filo pastry
40 g/1¹/₂ oz butter, melted
280 g/10 oz cherry tomatoes
100 g/3¹/₂ oz ricotta cheese

2 tbsp olive oil
2 garlic cloves, crushed
Handful of fresh basil leaves
Salt and ground black pepper

Preheat the oven to 180°C/350°C/Gas Mark 4. Grease a baking sheet. Lay one sheet of filo pastry on a board and brush with melted butter, lay a second sheet on top and brush with more butter. Place a quarter of the tomatoes in the centre of the filo. Add dollops of ricotta, nestled around and among the tomatoes.

Gather the filo around the filling and twist the edges together to make an open tart with a firm collar around the edge. Combine the oil and garlic and drizzle this over the tomatoes and ricotta. Season with salt and pepper.

Repeat with the remaining filo sheets and filling to make three more tartlets. Bake for 15 minutes, until crisp and golden. Serve immediately, sprinkled with fresh basil leaves.

Serves 4

roast butternut squash soup with char-grilled chillies

see variations page 277

This sweet, fragrant, lightly spiced soup makes a wonderful appetiser – particularly in the cooler autumn and winter months when squash are in season.

1 butternut squash, halved and seeded
2 tbsp olive oil, plus extra for brushing
Salt and ground black pepper
4 mild green chillies, halved and seeded
1 onion, chopped
2 garlic cloves, chopped

1 tsp ground cumin
1 tsp ground coriander
$1/2$ tsp ground ginger
$1/4$ tsp ground cinnamon
1.2 litres/2 pints vegetable or chicken stock
Juice of $1/2$ lemon

Preheat the oven to 200°C/400°F/Gas Mark 6. Brush the cut side of the squash with oil and season, then place on a baking sheet and roast for about 30 minutes, until tender.

Preheat a griddle pan or grill. Brush the chillies with oil and cook on both sides for about 4 minutes, until charred. Cut into strips and set aside. Fry the onion and garlic in the rest of the oil for 5 minutes. Add the ground spices and stock, and bring to the boil. Reduce the heat, cover and simmer for 15 minutes. Scoop the flesh from the squash into the soup. Purée until smooth in a blender. Reheat the soup, and add lemon juice and seasoning to taste.

To serve, ladle the soup into bowls and scatter strips of char-grilled chilli over the top.

Serves 4

oysters with red onion, mint & cucumber vinaigrette

see variations page 278

Oysters have a salty, satisfying flavour and add a touch of panache to any meal.

¹/₄ red onion, finely diced
¹/₄ cucumber, seeded and finely diced
2 tsp red wine vinegar
2 tbsp olive oil

Pinch of sugar
2 tsp chopped fresh mint
12 freshly shucked oysters in the shell
Salt and ground black pepper

Put the onion and cucumber in a bowl and pour over the vinegar and oil. Sprinkle with the sugar and season with salt and pepper, then stir to combine. Fold in the mint and taste to check the seasoning.

Arrange the oysters on a plate, spoon the dressing over them and serve immediately.

Serves 4

courgette pancakes with tomato salsa

see variations page 279

These deliciously tender, creamy pancakes look stunning topped with a rich red tomato salsa. Make your own salsa or use the recipe on page 51.

2 courgettes, trimmed
$^1/_4$ tsp salt
2 tbsp self-raising flour
2 egg yolks
3 tbsp double cream

2 spring onions, finely sliced
25 g/1 oz freshly grated Parmesan cheese
Olive oil, for frying
Ground black pepper
Tomato salsa, to serve

Grate the courgettes, sprinkle with the salt and toss to combine. Place in a colander or sieve and leave to drain over a bowl for 30 minutes.

Put the flour in a bowl. Add the egg yolks and cream, and whisk with a fork until smooth. Squeeze as much liquid out of the courgettes as possible, then add them to the batter with the spring onions and Parmesan. Season with pepper and fold together until combined.

Heat a non-stick frying pan and add a drizzle of olive oil. Add tablespoonfuls of mixture, shaping them into round pancakes. Fry gently for about 3 minutes on each side, until firm and golden. Keep warm while you cook the remaining mixture. Serve the pancakes warm, topped with spoonfuls of tomato salsa.

Serves 4

mussels in white wine

see variations page 280

Mussels look impressive, yet they are incredibly easy to cook. There's also something incredibly sensual about them that can't help but stimulate your appetite.

900 g/2 lb mussels, cleaned
28 g/1 oz butter
2 garlic cloves, finely chopped
120 ml/4 fl oz white wine

2 tbsp double cream
2 tbsp chopped fresh parsley
Salt and ground black pepper
French bread, to serve

Check the mussels and discard any that are open and do not shut when tapped. Melt the butter in a large saucepan and gently fry the garlic for about 1 minute.

Add the mussels, pour the wine over them, cover the pan tightly and cook for about 5 minutes over a fairly high heat, until the mussels have opened.

Lift the mussels into four serving bowls using a slotted spoon. Discard any that have not opened. Stir the cream and parsley into the cooking liquor and season to taste. Pour over the mussels and serve with crusty French bread.

Serves 4

red onion & parmesan tartlets

see variations page 281

These simple tartlets are stunning. To prepare them ahead, make the custard and cut out the pastry in advance, then assemble and bake the tartlets at the last minute.

60 ml/2 fl oz milk
60 ml/2 fl oz single cream
2 garlic cloves, peeled and halved
1 egg yolk
$1/2$ tbsp plain flour
28 g/1 oz freshly grated Parmesan cheese
Salt and ground black pepper

250 g/9 oz puff pastry
2 red onions, cut into 6 to 8 wedges each
1 tsp capers, rinsed
$1/4$ tsp balsamic vinegar
1 tsp olive oil
2 tsp chopped fresh parsley

Preheat the oven to 190°C/375°F/Gas Mark 5. Grease a baking sheet. Bring the milk, cream and garlic to the boil in a pan, then leave to cool for about 15 minutes. Discard the garlic. Whisk the egg yolk and flour to a paste. Bring the milk back to simmering point, then pour it into the paste, whisking until smooth. Return to the pan and heat gently for 4 to 5 minutes, stirring, until thick and creamy. Remove from the heat, stir in the cheese and season to taste.

Roll out the pastry and cut out four 12-cm/4$1/2$-in rounds. Place on the baking sheet and spread the cheese custard over them, leaving a 0.5 to 1-cm/$1/4$ to$1/2$-in border around the edge. Arrange about 3 onion wedges on each tart, then sprinkle capers around them. Whisk the vinegar with the oil and drizzle this over the onions. Bake for 15 to 20 minutes, until golden. Serve hot, warm or at room temperature, sprinkled with fresh parsley.

Serves 4

chicken liver pâté with garlic toasts

see variations page 282

Smooth rich chicken liver pâté is utterly irresistible and perfect for entertaining because you can make it in advance, then forget about it until you're ready to sit down to eat.

115 g/4 oz butter
2 garlic cloves, crushed
400 g/14 oz chicken livers, trimmed and
    chopped
2 tbsp brandy
$1/2$ tsp fresh thyme leaves
Salt and ground black pepper

for the toasts

8 baguette slices

1 garlic clove, halved
Olive oil, for drizzling

Melt 25g/1 oz of the butter in a non-stick pan and fry the garlic gently for 1 minute. Add the chicken livers and cook for about 5 minutes, until browned, then transfer to a food processor, with all the butter from the pan.

Add the remaining butter, brandy and thyme, and process until smooth. Season to taste and transfer to a bowl. Cover and chill for at least 2 hours or until firm.

To serve, toast the baguette slices on both sides until golden. Rub each slice with the cut garlic clove and drizzle with a little olive oil. Serve with the pâté.

Serves 4

roast peppers with cherry tomatoes, ricotta & pesto

see variations page 283

Serve these simple roast peppers with chunks of crusty white bread for mopping up the juices. For a light starter, halve the recipe and serve half a pepper per person.

2 tbsp green pesto
2 tbsp olive oil
285 g/10 oz cherry tomatoes, halved
285-g/10-oz jar char-grilled artichoke hearts,
    drained and cut into bite-size pieces

2 red peppers, halved and seeded
2 yellow peppers, halved and seeded
175 g/6 oz ricotta cheese
Ground black pepper

Preheat the oven to 200°C/400°F/Gas Mark 6. Combine the pesto and olive oil, then add the tomatoes and artichokes, and fold together to coat the vegetables well.

Arrange the peppers in a baking dish and divide the tomato and artichoke mixture among them. Add dollops of ricotta. Drizzle with any remaining oil and pesto, and grind black pepper over.

Bake for about 30 minutes, until the peppers are tender and the filling is bubbling. Serve hot or warm.

Serves 4

variations

vichyssoise with sour cream & chives

see base recipe page 255

hot leek & potato soup
Prepare the basic recipe, but serve hot instead of chilled.

plain & simple vichyssoise with ice cubes
Prepare the basic recipe, adding a couple of ice cubes to each bowl of soup and omitting the sour cream and chives.

vichyssoise with toasted baguette
Prepare the basic recipe. To serve, combine 4 tablespoons crème fraîche with 1 tablespoon snipped fresh chives. Halve two small baguettes and toast them until crisp and golden. Spread with the crème fraîche mixture and serve immediately with the soup.

vichyssoise with herb pitta toasts
Prepare the basic recipe. To serve, split 4 pitta breads in half and grill on both sides until crisp and golden. Drizzle with olive oil and sprinkle with chopped fresh parsley and serve.

vichyssoise with red onion
Prepare the basic recipe and sprinkle the finished soup with finely diced red onion instead of the chives.

marinated seared scallops

see base recipe page 257

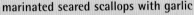

marinated seared scallops with garlic
Prepare the basic recipe, adding 1 crushed garlic clove to the marinade.

marinated seared scallops with ginger
Prepare the basic recipe, adding 1 teaspoon grated fresh root ginger to
the marinade.

marinated seared scallops with fresh basil
Prepare the basic recipe, sprinkling the scallops with torn fresh basil leaves
before serving.

marinated seared scallops with fresh coriander
Prepare the basic recipe, sprinkling the scallops with 1 tablespoon chopped
fresh coriander leaves before serving.

variations

filo tartlets with cherry tomatoes, basil & ricotta

see base recipe page 258

filo tartlets with cherry tomatoes & roast peppers
Prepare the basic recipe, adding strips of roast pepper to the filling.

filo tartlets with cherry tomatoes & chives
Prepare the basic recipe, sprinkling the cooked tartlets with 1 to 2 tablespoons snipped fresh chives in place of the basil.

filo tartlets with cherry tomatoes, basil & blue cheese
Prepare the basic recipe, using crumbled blue cheese in place of the ricotta.

filo tartlets with cherry tomatoes, basil & goat's cheese
Prepare the basic recipe, using cubed goat's cheese in place of the ricotta.

filo tartlets with cherry tomatoes, rocket & ricotta
Prepare the basic recipe, serving the tartlets topped with a handful of fresh rocket leaves in place of the basil.

variations

roast butternut squash soup with char-grilled chillies

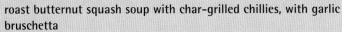

see base recipe page 261

roast butternut squash soup with char-grilled chillies, with garlic bruschetta
Prepare the basic recipe. Toast 8 baguette slices on both sides, then rub with a cut garlic clove, drizzle with oil and serve with the soup.

roast butternut squash soup with sour cream and char-grilled chillies
Prepare the basic recipe, adding a dollop of sour cream to each bowl of soup, and sprinkling with the chillies before serving.

roast beetroot soup with char-grilled chilllies
Prepare the basic recipe, using 3 large, peeled beetroots cut into wedges in place of the squash.

roast pumpkin soup with char-grilled chillies
Prepare the basic recipe, using a large wedge of pumpkin in place of the butternut squash.

variations

oysters with red onion, mint & cucumber vinaigrette

see base recipe page 262

oysters with shallot & tarragon vinaigrette
Prepare the basic recipe, using $1/2$ finely chopped shallot in place of the red onion, and chopped fresh tarragon in place of the mint.

oysters with red onion & tomato vinaigrette
Prepare the basic recipe, using 1 finely chopped, seeded tomato in place of the cucumber.

oysters with spring onion & chilli vinaigrette
Prepare the basic recipe, using 2 finely chopped spring onions in place of the red onion, and a good pinch of dried chilli flakes.

oysters with red onion & green pepper vinaigrette
Prepare the basic recipe, using $1/2$ finely diced green pepper in place of the cucumber.

variations

courgette pancakes with tomato salsa

see base recipe page 265

courgette pancakes with sour cream & chives
Prepare the basic recipe, topping the pancakes with a dollop of sour cream and a sprinkling of snipped fresh chives instead of tomato salsa.

courgette pancakes with sour cream & caviar
Prepare the basic recipe, topping each pancake with a dollop of sour cream and a teaspoonful of caviar.

courgette pancakes with pesto cream
Stir 2 teaspoon pesto into 75 ml/2^{1}/$_{2}$ fl oz crème fraîche and season with black pepper. Prepare the basic recipe and top the pancakes with the pesto cream instead of salsa.

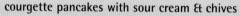

courgette pancakes with tomato salsa & avocado
Prepare the basic recipe, topping the pancakes with tomato salsa and slices of ripe avocado.

courgette pancakes with tomato salsa & sour cream
Prepare the basic recipe and top each pancake with a spoonful of salsa and a spoonful of sour cream.

variations

mussels in white wine

see base recipe page 266

mussels in beer
Prepare the basic recipe, using a light beer in place of the wine and omitting the cream.

mussels in white wine with blue cheese
Prepare the basic recipe, using 2 finely chopped shallots in place of the garlic, and stirring 40 g/1$\frac{1}{2}$ oz crumbled blue cheese into the cooking liquor in place of the cream.

mussels with sherry & chorizo
Prepare the basic recipe, adding 28 g/1 oz finely chopped chorizo to the butter with the garlic, and using sherry in place of the white wine. Omit the cream.

mussels in white wine with garlic & chilli
Prepare the basic recipe, adding $\frac{1}{4}$ teaspoon dried chilli flakes with the garlic.

red onion & parmesan tartlets

see base recipe page 269

red onion & parmesan tartlets with olives
Prepare the basic recipe, adding a couple of black olives to each tart.

red onion & parmesan tartlets with pine nuts
Prepare the basic recipe, sprinkling over 1 tablespoon pine nuts before baking the tartlets.

red onion, parmesan & prosciutto tartlets
Tear 4 wafer-thin slices of prosciutto into pieces. Prepare the basic recipe and nestle pieces of prosciutto among the wedges of onion before baking.

red onion, parmesan & chive tartlets
Prepare the basic recipe, stirring 1 tablespoon snipped fresh chives into the custard. Sprinkle with more fresh chives, instead of parsley, before serving.

variations

chicken liver pâté with garlic toasts

see base recipe page 270

duck liver pâté with garlic toasts
Prepare the basic recipe, using duck livers in place of the chicken livers.

sherried chicken liver pâté with garlic toasts
Prepare the basic recipe, using sherry in place of the brandy.

chicken liver & chive pâté with garlic toasts
Prepare the basic recipe, stirring 1 tablespoon snipped chives into the blended pâté before chilling. Serve sprinkled with more chives.

chicken liver & oregano pâté with garlic toasts
Prepare the basic recipe, using oregano in place of the thyme

chicken liver pâté with toasted sourdough
Prepare the basic recipe, serving the pâté with slices of toasted sourdough bread instead of the garlic toasts.

variations

roast peppers with cherry tomatoes, ricotta & pesto

see base recipe page 273

roast peppers with cherry tomatoes, mascarpone & pesto
Prepare the basic recipe, using mascarpone in place of the ricotta.

roast peppers with cherry tomatoes, mozzarella & pesto
Cut 150 g/5^1/$_2$ oz mozzarella into bite-size pieces and prepare the basic recipe using the mozzarella in place of the ricotta.

roast peppers with cherry tomatoes, goat's cheese & pesto
Prepare the basic recipe, using cubes of goat's cheese in place of the ricotta.

roast peppers with cherry tomatoes, jalepenos & pesto
Prepare the basic recipe, adding 2 sliced, bottled jalepenos to the tomato and artichoke mixture.

index

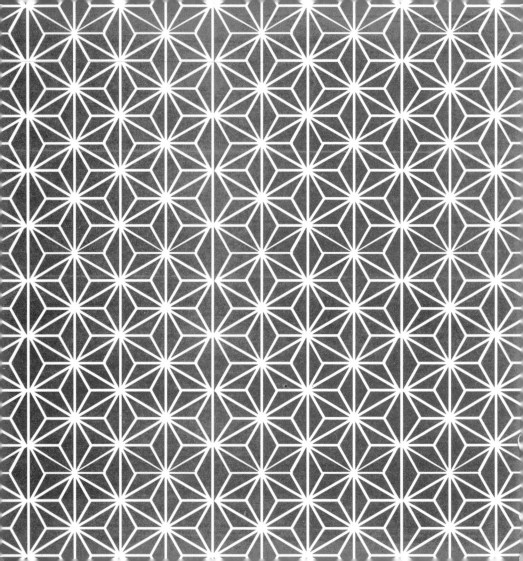